Anecdote Research

BLOOMSBURY RESEARCH METHODS

Edited by Mark Elliot and Jessica Nina Lester

The Bloomsbury Research Methods series provides authoritative introductions to key and emergent research methods across a range of disciplines.

Each book introduces the key elements of a particular method and/or methodology and includes examples of its application. Written in an accessible style by leading experts in the field, this series is an innovative pedagogical and research resource.

Also available in the series
Community Studies, Graham Crow
Diary Method, Ruth Bartlett and Christine Milligan
Embodied Inquiry, Jennifer Leigh and Nicole Brown
GIS, Nick Bearman
Inclusive Research, Melanie Nind
Mixed Methods Research, Donna M. Mertens
Narrative Research, Molly Andrews, Mark Davis, Cigdem Esin, Barbara Harrison, Lars-Christer Hydén, Margareta Hydén, Aura Lounasmaa and Corinne Squire
Online Research, Tristram Hooley and Rachel Buchanan
Qualitative Interviewing, 2nd edition, Rosalind Edwards and Janet Holland
Qualitative Longitudinal Research, Bren Neale
Quantitative Longitudinal Data Analysis, Vernon Gayle and Paul Lambert
Rhythmanalysis, Dawn Lyon
Social Network Analysis, John Scott
Vignette Research, Evi Agostini, Michael Schratz and Irma Eloff

Forthcoming in the series
Statistical Modelling in R, Kevin Ralston, Vernon Gayle, Roxanne Connelly and Chris Playford

Anecdote Research

Research Methods

**HANS KARL PETERLINI AND
GABRIELE RATHGEB**

BLOOMSBURY ACADEMIC
LONDON • NEW YORK • OXFORD • NEW DELHI • SYDNEY

BLOOMSBURY ACADEMIC
Bloomsbury Publishing Plc

Bloomsbury Publishing Plc, 50 Bedford Square, London, WC1B 3DP, UK
Bloomsbury Publishing Inc, 1385 Broadway, New York, NY 10018, USA
Bloomsbury Publishing Ireland, 29 Earlsfort Terrace, Dublin 2, D02 AY28, Ireland

BLOOMSBURY, BLOOMSBURY ACADEMIC and the Diana logo are trademarks of Bloomsbury Publishing Plc

First published in Great Britain 2025

Copyright © Hans Karl Peterlini and Gabriele Rathgeb, 2025

Hans Karl Peterlini and Gabriele Rathgeb have asserted their right under the Copyright, Designs and Patents Act, 1988, to be identified as Authors of this work.

For legal purposes the Acknowledgements on p. x constitute an extension of this copyright page.

Series design: Charlotte James
Cover image © shuoshu / iStock

This work is published open access subject to a Creative Commons Attribution 4.0 licence (CC BY 4.0, https://creativecommons.org/licenses/by/4.0/). You may re-use, distribute, reproduce, and adapt this work in any medium, including for commercial purposes, provided you give attribution to the copyright holder and the publisher, provide a link to the Creative Commons licence, and indicate if changes have been made.

Bloomsbury Publishing Plc does not have any control over, or responsibility for, any third-party websites referred to or in this book. All internet addresses given in this book were correct at the time of going to press. The author and publisher regret any inconvenience caused if addresses have changed or sites have ceased to exist, but can accept no responsibility for any such changes.

A catalogue record for this book is available from the British Library.

A catalog record for this book is available from the Library of Congress.

ISBN: HB: 978-1-3503-3679-7
PB: 978-1-3503-3678-0
ePDF: 978-1-3503-3681-0
eBook: 978-1-3503-3680-3

Series: Bloomsbury Research Methods

Typeset by Newgen KnowledgeWorks Pvt. Ltd., Chennai, India
Printed and bound in Great Britain

For product safety related questions contact productsafety@bloomsbury.com.

To find out more about our authors and books visit www.bloomsbury.com and sign up for our newsletters.

CONTENTS

List of figures vii
Series editors' foreword viii
Acknowledgements x
Notes on translation xi

Introduction 1

Part I Understanding anecdote research

1 What is anecdote research? 5
2 History and positioning to similar approaches 23
3 Theoretical foundations and implications for practice 31

Part II Doing anecdote research

4 Starting research with conversations and interviews 55
5 From transcript to anecdote 73
6 Resonance reading and reflecting upon anecdotes 85

Part III Potentials of anecdote research and outlook

7 Examples of applications in different research fields and contexts 119
8 Looking back and ahead 139

References 143
Index 157

FIGURES

1 Circle 39
2 Square 39
3 Face 40
4 Unregular Shape 40
5 Perception 40

SERIES EDITORS' FOREWORD

The idea behind this book series is a simple one: to provide concise and accessible introductions to frequently used research methodologies and methods, as well as to current issues in research methodology. Books in the series have been written by experts in their fields with a request to write about their subject for a broad audience.

The series has been developed through a partnership between Bloomsbury and the UK's National Centre for Research Methods (NCRM). The original 'what is' series emerged from the eponymous strand at NCRM's popular Research Methods Festivals, which began in 2004 and moved online in 2021 and 2023 for its ninth and tenth runs.

This relaunched series reflects changes in the research landscape, embracing research methods innovation and interdisciplinarity. Methodological innovation is the order of the day, and the books provide updates to the latest developments while still maintaining an emphasis on accessibility to a wide audience. The format allows researchers who are new to a field to gain an insight into its key features, while also providing a useful update on recent developments for people who have had some prior acquaintance with it. All readers should find it helpful to be taken through the discussion of key terms, the history of how the method or methodological issue has developed and the assessment of the strengths and possible weaknesses of the approach through analysis of illustrative examples.

In *Anecdote Research*, Hans Karl Peterlini and Gabriele Rathgeb introduce readers to anecdote research, describing it as a method that serves to expand how researchers might study lifeworld phenomena and experiences. Notably, the authors point to the limits of many existing methods that focus on the study of human experience. They note that many such methods do not fully account for the '(inter)human experience'. In contrast, anecdote research – which is grounded in phenomenology – attends to 'atmospheric and bodily phenomena' and thus seeks to more fully consider bodily expressions evidenced in the data.

Across the book's seven chapters, Peterlini and Rathgeb introduce both the theoretical basis of the anecdotal methods and concrete practices associated with them. The book is structured into two parts, with the first three chapters providing a foundational overview and the remaining chapters providing concrete guidance on designing and carrying out anecdote research. As the authors note in the initial chapters, this method was developed at the University of Innsbruck in Austria alongside vignette research. The historical trajectory of anecdotal research provides insights on how it came to be and the assumptions it espouses; thus, unsurprisingly, the authors begin the book with a general overview of the origins of the method. Chapter 3 offers a deeper overview of the theoretical perspectives that undergird anecdote research. In Chapters 4 through 6, the authors introduce readers to core considerations for designing and carrying out anecdote research. This includes considering how and why to collect conversations and interview data, as well as the central analytic practices. Usefully, Chapter 7 provides multiple exemplars and, in so doing, illustrates the range of research foci that researchers using this method might have. Indeed, as the authors illustrate, this method opens new pathways for researchers focused on experience-based research.

While the books within this series do not provide information about their subject matter down to a fine level of detail, they do equip readers with a sense of the reasons why methods, such as anecdote research, are worth careful study. This book is no exception. Here, the authors provide a compelling and innovative overview for readers interested in taking up anecdote research.

Jessica Nina Lester and Mark Elliot

ACKNOWLEDGEMENTS

We would like to thank all the people who contributed to this book:
- the colleagues in our research community who contributed significantly to the development of Anecdote Research, especially Silvia Krenn and Michael Schratz,
- our colleagues who wrote some of the anecdotes included in this book: Jasmin Donlic, Markus Ammann, Silvia Krenn, Annemarie Winder, Daniela Lehner,
- Rachel Wallace, who did the English proofreading and formatting of the text, an essential contribution to presenting our research approach in a concise way and making it understandable for readers,
- Michael Schratz for his feedback as a critical friend,
- Laura Gallon and Ben Piggott, who provided us with information and whose enquiries helped us to stay on schedule after all.

We would also like to thank our partners and families for their support and for understanding our temporary (mental) absence.

Anecdote Research was published with the support of the Austrian Science Fund (FWF): Grant-DOI: 10.55776/PUB 1173 Research results from: Austrian Science Fund (FWF): P 22230-G17 and P 25373-G16

NOTES ON TRANSLATION

DeepL and Grammarly were helpful with the translations. All emphases correspond to the original, unless otherwise stated.

Introduction

Dear Reader,

As you have picked up this book, we assume you are interested in qualitative research methods suitable for describing lifeworlds from the inside, from the perspective of those actively involved.

In particular, research into lifeworld phenomena and experiences requires continuous searching for suitable procedures and methods. Using data collection and analysis methods, researchers often experience that significant aspects of (inter)human experience fall by the wayside. These aspects can be perceived and sensed via observation or interviews but cannot be fully captured by conventional analysis methods.

This dissatisfaction was the impetus for the emergence of anecdote research. In anecdotes, data obtained through conversations or interviews are condensed into narratives. Atmospheric and bodily phenomena expressed in conversation are included as essential facets of recalled experiences. This specificity is based on a phenomenological understanding of (inter)subjectivity and inter-corporeality (Merleau-Ponty 1994), manifesting as reciprocal responses in a conversational situation. Thus, the method makes it possible to give space to that pathic surplus in the narratives without prematurely defining the stream of experience in the verbalization and disambiguation.

The theoretical basis for the anecdote research is phenomenology. The different approaches of this school of thought are united by the concern to capture experiences in their bodily, temporal, spatial, relational and power-shaped dimensions at the moment of their emergence (*in statu nascendi*) and to describe them both theoretically and empirically. One characteristic of phenomenology is the differentiation and theoretical complexity of studies on human references to the other and others (Rathgeb 2023: 443).

In Chapter 1 of Part I, we introduce the anecdote as a research instrument (1.1) and discuss its essential characteristics (1.2). Chapter 2 describes the history of the method's development (2.1) and the similarities and differences to related approaches (2.2). Chapter 3 deepens the theoretical and epistemological foundations of anecdote research. What ensures its validity, and what justifies the approach? Part II introduces anecdote research step by step in a very concrete way. First, we go into detail about how researchers should prepare for interviews or situations where interesting impromptu conversations are likely to occur, and what attitude they should adopt during the interviews (Chapter 4). Chapter 5 introduces anecdote writing and explains how to edit transcribed interviews and conversations.

The question of how anecdotes are interpreted and reflected upon to gain insights from them is addressed in Chapter 6. Here, we present various forms of reading and invite readers to experiment with them. Finally, Chapter 7 of Part III outlines specific potential applications, providing insight into experiences working with anecdotes and specific research projects. Chapter 8 concludes with an outlook on possible future developments of this young approach. It encourages readers to engage with the method and thus contribute to its further development.

We are confident that anecdote research expands the range of methods of experience-orientated research. However, the anecdote is not only applicable as a research method. Still, it can also be used fruitfully in the training and further education of professionals in various fields and organizational development.

According to a phenomenological understanding, learning is always a relearning process that draws on our previous experiences and assumptions as well as on prior practical and theoretical knowledge but simultaneously makes this horizon thematic and questionable. With this in mind, may your reading confirm and occasionally expand your experiences and expertise.

PART I

Understanding anecdote research

CHAPTER 1

What is anecdote research?

Anecdote research is a special and still developing research approach that was developed at the University of Innsbruck (Austria) along with so-called vignette research (see Agostini, Eloff and Schratz 2024). It is now spreading to various research centres in and outside Europe.[1] Vignette and anecdote research are part of the diverse range of phenomenological research approaches (see Peterlini 2020a). While vignettes, in short, are dense descriptions of co-experienced events,[2] anecdotes serve to recover, reflect on and interpret recalled experiences. Anecdote research combines the informative value of a particular type of narrative interview or conversation with the perception of body expressions during the interviews. In the evaluation and processing of the contents of the conversations, meaningful verbally expressed passages and the observed speaking of the body are brought together and condensed in a new way to form short, pointed anecdotes, which are then subjected to an in-depth reflection and multifaceted interpretation of what has been said.

To introduce this method, the first section of this chapter will argue the significance of anecdotes as a qualitative research method. Based on this, the second section explains the main features of anecdote research and the essential characteristics of the anecdote.

1.1 Anecdotes as scholarly tools

Etymology and definition of the term

Anecdotes are not generally associated with research. Etymologically, the term comes from the Ancient Greek ἀνέκδοτος (*anékdotos*) for 'unpublished' and has acquired the meaning of a 'secret history'. The term appeared prominently in the title of the memoirs of the private lives of the Eastern Roman imperial couple Justinian and Theodora, which were not intended for publication (Onions 1969: 36). The *Oxford English Dictionary* [3] adds three contemporary developments to the historical meaning. The first is 'a short account of an amusing, interesting, or telling incident or experience', accordingly characterized by 'superficiality or unreliability', which does not exactly speak in favour of the empirical quality of the anecdote. Added to this is the meaning of 'writing, content, or information consisting of short interesting, amusing, etc., accounts', distinguished from high-quality literature. Finally, an anecdote could be an art piece depicting a minor narrative incident. These definitions correspond to the perception in other language areas. In German-language literary studies, the anecdote belongs to the miniature epic forms, mostly passed on orally (Gutzen, Oellers and Petersen 1981: 41) and characterized by a simple structure.

The German Dictionary of the Brothers Grimm[4] denies the anecdote any literary value. It defines them as 'little stories', usually unauthenticated (vol. 2: 838, line 57).

The paradigmatic framing

What methodological validity can an anecdote claim at all when it is measured against reliability, validity and objectivity (see Adams 1936) as the primarily recognized quality criteria? To answer this question, we need to clarify the scholarly paradigm in which anecdote research is situated. An understanding of academia that only recognizes propositional forms of knowledge, such as most measuring and quantifying disciplines and conventional natural sciences, separates objectively verifiable knowledge from knowledge that cannot be objectively validated and confirmed (see Gabriel 2010: 43). An understanding of evidence as intersubjectively shared experience is positioned supplementarily to that 'knowledge that' (or 'knowledge of what the case is') (see Husserl [1931] 1982: 284). While propositional knowledge can usually be determined as true or false (see Gabriel 2010: 45), paradigms that focus on non-propositional forms of knowledge are orientated towards the scholarly validity of sensory perception, including subjective and intersubjective experience. Such an understanding of knowledge does not reduce reality to true or false but differentiates it in its ambivalence and multifacetedness. Trusting in the human capacity for empathy and understanding, an understanding of science that also includes non-propositional forms of knowledge also legitimizes methods that generate knowledge about people and the world from subjective narratives and artistic forms of expression (see Denzin and Lincoln 2008; Savin-Baden and Wimpenny 2014). The anecdote, as described in the approach of the methodology outlined here, is understood as an intersubjectively interpreted narrative of remembered subjective experiences.

Interestingly, even in the propositional science paradigm, anecdotes are not wholly denied their scholarly validity. For example, Lilienfeld, Lynn and Lohr (2014: 8) concede that 'testimonial and anecdotal evidence can be quite useful in the early stages of academic investigation'. Anecdotal evidence cannot prove or disprove hypotheses, but it can generate them. Macnaughton (1995: 571) goes even further in explaining how vital individual case studies and anecdotes can be for the training of medical staff: 'Clinical medical teaching is done on an apprentice basis where the experience of the teacher is handed down largely by anecdotes. ... From seeing people as homogeneous (in the scientific preclinical year of the course) students learn the reality of medical practice through the experience relayed in narrative by teachers and patients alike' (ibid.). Accordingly, anecdotes are also common in the professional development, evaluation and coaching of teams, as well as the research, reflection and optimization of work and group processes (see Bell 1994). Anecdotes are just as favoured as they are suitable for depicting epochs and developments in historical studies (see Gossmann 2003) and for visualizing social situations in the social and human sciences. Dahlstrom thus turns the famous mantra 'The plural of anecdote is not data', which is sceptical towards anecdotes, into a positive variant: 'The plural of anecdote is engaging science communication' (Dahlstrom 2014: 13618).

In the tradition of Aristotle

The non-propositional understanding of science in vignette and anecdote research correspondingly sees the anecdote as having the potential to generate scholarly knowledge. Regarding the history of ideas, the appreciation of the anecdote as a meaningful statement about reality goes back to Aristotle's epagogy (επαγωγή, *epagōgē*), which is still considered the basis for inductive methods of cognition today. Aristotle seems to favour the style of deduction (Thompson 1975: 81) in which conclusions are derived from general, testable hypotheses and applied to individual cases. Nevertheless, with induction, he also opened up the reverse path of cognition to infer the general from the particular case. The single case is understood as an example of the general, in which traces of the universal can be inductively found and plausibly established through the human faculty of understanding (*nous*): 'Aristotle indicates that through *epagōgē* and *nous*, one comes to grasp (*noēsai*) relevant universal propositions' (Upton 1981: 174). Aristotle attributes academic plausibility to the in-depth, reason-guided examination of the individual case as an example of the universal, thanks to man's intuitive abilities (ibid.: 175).

Arrighetti (2007) builds upon this, analysing anecdotes in ancient biographies, particularly those of Aristotle. He defines the anecdote as a short narrative of an event that is not particularly significant in itself but capable of 'assuming great importance' (ibid.: 79–80). Arrighetti refers to Nietzsche (1973 [1873]), who even considered it possible and legitimate to draw a picture of a person from three anecdotes (297).

Max van Manen, who conceived and established the anecdote for phenomenology as a 'methodological device' (van Manen 1989: 232), cites two historical examples to thematize the epistemological content of anecdotes. One concerns the founder of phenomenology, Edmund Husserl himself: 'As a boy, Husserl wanted to sharpen his knife. And he persisted in making the knife sharper and sharper until finally he had nothing left' (ibid.: 244, quoted from de Boer 1980: 10).

For van Manen, this amusing episode is an early indication of the later life's work of Husserl, 'whose voluminous writing on phenomenology contain painstaking refutations of every conceivable objection to his philosophical system' (ibid.). In his tireless writing, Husserl endeavoured to sharpen and hone his ideas – metaphorically, his pencils – to defend himself against metaphysical definitions of reality, thus exposing himself to nothingness in conventional notions of ontology. The second example concerns the Greek philosopher Diogenes Laertius, of whom no texts remain as a legacy. Only anecdotes tell of him. One of the most famous is about an encounter between the philosopher, who was supposedly living in a barrel and dressed in rags, and Alexander the Great:

Anecdote 1

Alexander: I am Alexander the Great.
Diogenes: I am Diogenes, the dog.
Alexander: The dog?
Diogenes: I nuzzle the kind, bark at the greedy, and bite louts.
Alexander: What can I do for you?
Diogenes: Stand out of my light. (Ibid., quoted from de Boer 1980: 30)

Contemporary philosophers and historians attach great importance to the anecdotes surrounding Diogenes, even claiming that they are 'more clarifying of his teachings than any writings could have been' (ibid.: 245). At the same time, van Manen surmises that 'the reason that Diogenes' philosophy has not been more influential may also find its cause in the fact that it is *only anecdotes* that have been preserved' (ibid., emphasis added).

Only anecdotes? Situated between a blind trust in the informative value of anecdotes and their rejection as trivial stories of no scholarly contribution, anecdote research adopts a stance of humility and self-confidence, with the recognition of the limits of its skill and the joyful exploration of its potential. More concretely, every method of handling and analysing data makes certain aspects of the same reality visible, inevitably leaving other aspects in the dark or haze. The area where anecdotal research sees its task corresponds to the genuine research field of phenomenology, namely the realm of experience. The speciality of the anecdote as an inductive tool lies in its ability to preserve experiences from the past for the present.

From lived to recalled experience

Based on Husserl, phenomenological research sees experience as the 'royal road to knowledge' (Peterlini et al. 2021: 109). Husserl's famous demand to go 'back to the "things themselves"' (Husserl 2001a [1900–1]: 168) is rooted in the context of his understanding of experience, through which humans have access to the world and the others. According to Husserl, 'natural knowledge starts with experience and remains in experience' (Husserl 2014 [1913]: 9). The phenomenological understanding of evidence is based on the 'self-appearance, the self-exhibiting, the self-giving of an affair, an affair complex (or state of affairs), a universality, a value, or other objectivity' to human consciousness (Husserl 1982 [1931]: 57). Thus, 'all evidence, we may say, is experience in a maximally broad, and yet essentially unitary, sense' (ibid.).

In a phenomenological understanding, lived experience is immediate and pre-reflective. We, therefore, only become aware of it retrospectively (Husserl 1991 [1928]: 132). Experience as ultimate cognition corresponds in Husserl's mind to a 'primal impressional stream of preconscious life that becomes interpretatively available to our understanding as lived experience', as Max van Manen (2007: 16) describes the phenomenological concept of experience. Phenomenological vignette research, for example, attempts to gain access to lived experiences *in statu nascendi* by allowing the researchers to be affected by perceived events in the field and initially sensing these as co-experienced experiences as free of interpretations as possible. Through this 'exercise of perception' (Peterlini, Cennamo and Donlic 2020: 7; Agostini et al. 2023; Agostini, Eloff and Schratz 2024), an attempt is made to avoid the hasty delineation of situations, subjects and acting persons into prefabricated categories by looking, listening and feeling closely and also being open to bodily speech. In the next step, the experienced perceptions are written down and condensed into concise vignettes to be fed into an undefined reflection and interpretation. In a further step, conclusions can be drawn on a general level based on vignettes and their interpretation.

This three-step process of perception, reflection and objectification corresponds to a requirement of Flores D'Arcais (1995; cf. Agostini et al. 2023: 10) for research interested to be in human learning and becoming. Statements of general value can be made through the perception of and subsequent reflection on individual situations. Research surrounding past experiences can only be concerned with how these manifest as memories in the present. How phenomena of remembering are related to those of forgetting is a complex question that Husserl dealt with intensively (see Chapter 3 for a more detailed discussion). Reference is made here to the related research interest of phenomenology, namely 'the investigation of the role of the phenomena of sedimentation, forgetfulness, and recollection in their constitution in the living present' (Hopkins 2023: 105).

One tool for capturing the constitution of memory in the present is the anecdote. Max van Manen has contributed fundamentally to establishing anecdotes in qualitative educational research. This particular form of anecdote describes personal experiences as closely as possible to what has been experienced. He draws his anecdotes primarily from 'closely observing situations' (van Manen 1990: 69). At the same time, however, he points out that 'personal experience and the interview … can also be sources for anecdotes' (ibid.).

Interviews, or rather conversations and impromptu narratives, as will be explained later, are the sources for the anecdote in the sense of phenomenological vignette and anecdote research. This limitation has to do with the fact that the description of lived experiences *in statu nascendi* in this research approach takes place through the vignette. The research experience with the vignette, in particular, has raised the question of how past experiences – that is, not lived but recalled experiences – can be traced phenomenologically. The basis for this is conversations with high narrative content, in which the researchers adopt a particular attitude of attention to perceive not only *what* is said and told but also the bodily *manner* of speaking. The researchers linguistically organize the content and scenic moments in the narrative form of the anecdote, as explained in more detail in the following chapters. The anecdote condenses what is spoken verbally, and physically in a meaningful way, expresses it comprehensibly and thus makes it available for reflection and interpretation.

Two features in particular make the anecdote seem suitable for this purpose:

1. Firstly, the incompleteness of narratives, which corresponds to the incompleteness of experiences. The narrative form

of the anecdote does not prematurely establish what cannot (yet) be found. Indeed, every verbalization always means a (provisional) recording of interpreting events and experiences. However, the characteristics of narratives make it possible to retain open gaps so that what is in flux or in-between can remain in limbo. The ambiguity of experiences is not, as in causal reconstructions, fixed to a single possible interpretation but rather remains open to the phenomenological 'excess' or 'surplus', which refers to the 'possible manifolds of perception' of the same thing (Husserl 2014: 79). According to Husserl, the endless process of meaning formation that is inherent in experience is absorbed without bringing it to a standstill (see Tengelyi 2007: 294). Narratives can be retold and heard or read again and again and filled with new meaning.

2. Secondly, the dramatic structure of narratives is an essential characteristic that Hogrebe describes as the 'primary [characteristic] for our perception of the world' (Hogrebe 2009: 50). The scenic quality of narratives corresponds to the multidimensionality of experiences. It makes it possible for readers or listeners to empathize with and experience narrated experiences, thanks to the sensuous quality of narrative texts, in which spatial, temporal, relational and bodily components flow together.

Several questions arise based on these anecdote characteristics: how can anecdotes be understood as research instruments? How do they emerge in the concrete research process? How are they processed and interpreted? How can insights be gained from them?

In the definition of the proposed research approach, an anecdote is a memorable and noteworthy (*merk-würdig*[5]) story which condenses events from the recalled experience of an interviewee with particular impact (see Rathgeb, Krenn and Schratz 2017: 130).

Anecdotes, as understood by phenomenological anecdote research, should have the characteristics *of an experience, a theme, a focus* and *a punchline*. As already mentioned, the basis are interviews or conversations and, subsequently, their recording through audio media and transcripts. The preference for conversation rather than interview indicates that researchers engage in a dialogue with research partners (see Chapter 4), in which the clear assignment of roles of interviewee and questioner is at least partially suspended. Subsequently, the method is also open for impromptu narratives, such as those developed by the Arbeitsgruppe Bielefelder Soziologen (1976) field research for explorations in public social space (Cennamo, Donlic and Peterlini 2020: 189).

1.2 Concepts and demarcations

Anecdote 2

> Heike has always been interested in history, and she had already been thinking about Mauthausen before the excursion. 'We were there now, and it was, it was, very intense', she whispers pensively: 'Are those still the cobblestones from that time?' Heike did not expect them to be. 'It is hard to imagine what was there', she concludes, thoughtfully falling silent. (Ammann et al. 2017: 190)

This example of an anecdote shows how different moments of the past and present moments of realization can merge into one another in the concise, pointed narrative form and how they can even develop together as something new. The pupil Heike tells us that she has always been interested in history and thought about it before the excursion with her school class to the former Mauthausen concentration camp. Presumably, the topic was already part of the curriculum, and the pupils had probably read up on it. This story of the past is one that can be taught as subject matter in class. However lively these lessons may be, they only reach the level of imagining incidents that are actually beyond the power of imagination. Heike then talks about her memories of the excursion. This level of the past now relates to her own experience, which she discusses in the interview. The force of the experience of standing at the site of the Nazi crimes hits her hard. Twice she begins to say that it was intense. The repetition 'it was, it was' expresses how she searches for words to express the unspeakable. In the memory of the encounter with the past, now experienced in reality, she can only whisper. The cobblestones in Mauthausen make the memory real. Her question as to whether they are really the stones from back then silences her completely, as if the suffering of the many victims is brought to life and at the same time becomes overwhelming with these silent witnesses. In the memory of the excursion experience, what was there then is no longer conceivable. Moreover, she now silences herself.

The anecdote may give a first impression of the methodological approach, the interest in knowledge and the potential of phenomenological anecdote research. The starting point for the anecdotes in the sense of the method proposed here are the stories, reports of experiences and reflections on the present and future of people as they manifest themselves in the present of the storytelling. In the sense of anecdote research, this can take place in interviews, focus groups, conversations or impromptu narratives.

Anecdote research is classed in a range of narrative methods without being wholly absorbed by them. The classic method for analysing human narratives is interviews of various kinds, including narrative interviews, semi-narrative or guided interviews and expert interviews. Interviews are usually recorded and then transcribed. For processing and analysing the data obtained in this way, researchers have various options based on specific theoretical approaches (e.g. constructivism, phenomenological lifeworld analysis, cultural studies, symbolic interactionism) and methodologies that more or less correspond to these. Well-known methods of analysis are qualitative content analysis, narrative hermeneutic analysis, in-depth hermeneutic analysis, grounded theory, documentary methods, and conversation and discourse analysis.

Brinkmann and Kvale distinguish between three groups of analysis methods: analyses focusing on meaning (meaning coding, meaning condensation, meaning interpretation), analyses focusing on language (linguistic analysis, conversation analysis, narrative analysis, discursive analysis, deconstruction), and bricolage (theoretical reading) (Brinkmann and Kvale 2018: 120). All these methods share the common aim to understand and describe social environments from the inside out by taking into account and incorporating the views and experiences of subjects, 'the subjective and social constructions of their world' (Flick 2012: 17).

Anecdotes represent a particular way of processing data obtained through interviews, focus groups, conversations or impromptu narratives, which are analysed and interpreted by *resonance readings* (see Chapter 6). This form of processing – in the sense of a mixed-method design – can also be combined with other methods.

The unique potential of anecdotes for tracking down remembered and narrated experiences is the subject of the following sections.

A plea in favour of storytelling and its importance for research

From the very beginning, we are not only surrounded by stories but enmeshed in stories (Schapp 2004). We develop an understanding of ourselves through the stories others tell about us and those we tell about ourselves. Stories help us make sense of what we experience and what happens to us and put events into context. A central dimension of stories is time. In stories, the temporal dimension of events and situations becomes tangible.

Stories, even the ones we tell about ourselves, are never just our own. They are nourished by a rich tradition of storytelling and by the narratives we recognize from our social, societal and political environment. Thus we adopt not only content but also narrative styles and linguistic and stylistic patterns. In storytelling, we can adopt content, themes and patterns according to the specific retelling. However, we can also change stories or turn away from conventional narratives altogether and tell new stories, including stories about ourselves.

When we tell stories, we understand connections better. As we tell stories or listen to them, many things become more apparent to us. Storytelling is a way of thinking, and knowledge is gained through storytelling. Philosophy, psychology, cultural studies and even the natural sciences are full of stories. Stories are used in psychotherapy to process traumatic experiences or to explore alternative courses of action. Religions also use stories to convey content, often stories about the founding figures or role models. Stories can have a healing, unifying and conciliatory effect, but they can also incite, discriminate and put people down. Stories can establish norms and confirm and reinforce attributions, but they can also question and break down rigid patterns and outdated rules and norms.

Storytelling is never just a monologue, even if speeches or stories by individuals may give this impression. Storytelling is always embedded in a communicative situation. A narrative is always a narrative for someone. It is associated with the expectation of feedback (Honnef-Becker and Kühn 2019: 63). Narratives – not only fictional ones – trigger joy, astonishment, relief or sympathy; they can generate amusement, fear or horror in listeners. The listeners help to shape the story, not just by interrupting or asking questions but simply by their presence, their response, their looks and gestures, their silence, clearing their throats or yawning. Consequently, the same story is never told in the same way twice. Voice, language and speech, gestures, posture and facial expressions, that is, body language, are used to tell stories.

However, you do not necessarily need a large vocabulary or extensive knowledge to tell stories. Even people with limited language skills or speech impediments can tell stories if they find empathetic listeners. This potential of stories is utilized in anecdote research to make remembered experiences resonate anew (see Chapter 3). As a form of narrative, the anecdote is appropriate to the expression of experience in that it *captures* the diverse process of meaning formation set in motion by it but does not prematurely fix it or even bring it to a standstill (see Tengelyi 2007: 294). However, we must reckon with the simplification of experience through narrative. This process can best be described through the image of a river: a cupful can be taken from the *river of experience*, and this water possibly has much of the quality of the river water and is even identical to it at that moment. At the same time, it is evident that the river or stream of experience is quite different from the water in the cup. It cannot be stopped and analysed, but rather we can only gain an insight into the experience by taking a part of it, putting it into a container and thereby giving it form and observing it more closely. It remains undisputed that other ways of accessing, expressing or communicating the flow of experience may exist. For example, it is possible to step into the river, swim along for a while, let oneself drift or sit at the river's edge and observe it (see Rathgeb, Krenn and Schratz 2017: 146).

From the interview to the phenomenologically orientated research conversation: Relationships and demarcations

Interviews are among the most frequently used data collection methods in qualitative research across all disciplines and contexts (see Brinkmann and Kvale 2018: xv). At the same time, the number of approaches and forms of interviews has become almost unmanageable in recent decades. These usually involve definite transcription rules and modes of recording.

Anecdote research speaks of *conversations* in the context of data collection and distinguishes this form from *interviews* (see Krenn 2020: 98–9). Van Manen (2007) also favours the conversational form: 'Perhaps it is better to think of the interview as a conversation than as "interview". Conversations require the right atmosphere and tone' (315). In his engagement with Schmitz's New Phenomenology, Griffero emphasizes the importance of the atmospheric for perception and relationship: 'Atmospheres are centripetal and external vectors; they have authority and, generating affective involvement (an embodied experience)' (Griffero 2019: 23; cf. Schmitz 1990: 310). *Doing conversation* means in this sense creating an atmospheric space and emphasizes the openness of the situation and researchers' efforts to conduct a conversation with the children and young people deserving of this name, that is, to enter into an interaction with them at eye level, in which the interviewees not only answer questions asked but also respond to claims in the sense of a question-answer process (Waldenfels 2007a) and – vice versa – questions can also be interpreted as answers to claims (cf. Rathgeb, Krenn and Schratz 2017: 139). 'Answering is … from the outset more than merely passing on existing knowledge, if only because an answer can be denied' (Waldenfels 2007a: 192). Such a response is not limited to the linguistic expression: when we hear a claim when something affects us and respond in this way, the body is inevitably involved. Taking this seriously not only means taking into account the extent to which responses are owed to the situation of the conversation, the role of the dialogue partners and their relationship to each other and the associated assumptions and (presumed) expectations but also means paying attention to all modes of responding: linguistic and non-linguistic, the sound of the voice as well as the gaze or facial expressions, posture as well as breathing or silence.

In anecdote research, this reciprocal response to the claims of the other in a research discussion is not a disruptance from which one should keep as much distance as possible. Instead, the researcher can use it as an additional source of insight. Therefore, the interviewers consciously practise an attitude that does not distance themselves from the interviewee but engages with them and is open to empathy and co-experience. Being able to co-experience the experience of others is a fundamental assumption of vignette and anecdote research (see Peterlini, Cennamo and Donlic 2020: 118). It is explained in more theoretical detail in Chapter 3.

To practise this attitude, researchers should be clear about their own prior experiences, assumptions and expectations so that they can put these – as well as prior knowledge and theoretical concepts – aside in the conversation and approach what is given and said as openly as possible.

Narrative elements are encouraged in phenomenologically orientated research discussions. However, the interviewees do not always tell stories. Van Manen (2007) regards a narrated story as a stroke of luck for research which rarely happens. He emphasizes that people remember and tell stories from their lives in a comfortable environment, sometimes at a coffee house or the kitchen table. The researcher needs trust, rapport and closeness to the interviewee. Good conversations take time, and short answers must be expected at the beginning of a conversation (see ibid.: 314).

How interviews and conversations are prepared, and the attitude with which they are conducted, is explained in more detail in Chapter 4. Readers will learn how narrated memories and fragmentary stories become anecdotes in Chapter 5.

The resonance of remembered experience

Anecdotes are written based on audio recordings and transcripts. The aim is not to produce a detailed reproduction but to condense the afflictive, disturbing, astonishing or surprising aspects of moments of dialogue in such a way that the experiences revealed in the conversation resonate anew and become understandable for readers. It is essential to record what is said and how something is said. Does a pupil stammer and falter when telling a story? Does she repeatedly fail to find the words, or do they just bubble out? Does she lower her head or look away? (See Peterlini, Cennamo and Donlic 2020: 118).

Capturing and representing lived experience in the form of phenomenological texts is an uncertain terrain and is constantly threatened with failure. This is not least due to the ambivalent, even paradoxical, relationship between lived experience and the expression thereof. It is no coincidence that one of van Manen's volumes is entitled *Writing in the Dark* (2002). Henriksson and Saevi also draw attention to the challenges of phenomenological writing: 'But there is no original meaning, just possible meanings and shadows on the wall of the cave, which we as researchers can try to describe, interpret, and bestow meaning upon' (Henriksson and Saevi 2009: 53).

Modesty is, therefore, appropriate for the claim to express experience (see Rathgeb, Krenn and Schratz 2017: 143). This also applies to the writing of anecdotes.

Phenomenological texts establish a connection between the lived experiences they evoke and the readers' experiences. As *events of sound* (cf. Henriksson and Saevi 2009: 53), they appeal to readers – to their hearing, to their thinking and to their bodies – and make it possible for lived experiences, also in their physical dimension, to be brought back to life during reading (see Rathgeb, Krenn and Schratz 2017: 142).

How to write anecdotes, how personal perceptions are brought into the text in terms of bodily interactivity during the interview and how the anecdote's theme, focus and punchline should be brought out will be explained in more detail in Chapter 5.

Anecdotes as traces to a general sense

One characteristic Arrighetti (2007) also ascribes to anecdotes with reference to Aristotle is their potential to refer to generalities. This characteristic also applies to the anecdote as a research instrument: we can understand the remembered experiences contained in the anecdotes as examples in which generalities emerge beyond the individual and can be experienced anew. It is essential not to presuppose the generalities. 'Examples do not subordinate themselves to a common generality like cases to a rule. Only by working through them does what is specifically general for them become recognizable' (Meyer-Drawe 2012: 15). Since it is not possible to transfer theory seamlessly into practice, and the functioning general is more, or different, than the conceptual general, examples become particularly significant when the meaning of something cannot (yet) be clearly determined and when non-propositional forms of knowledge must be included. As the general can first be traced in the concrete example, a productive approach to the theory-practice problem becomes possible (see Meyer-Drawe 1984: 256; referencing Agostini 2020: 169). Keeping the interpretation open also remains decisive for the next step: the interpretation of the texts in the form of *resonance readings*, which proceeds from a questioning attitude and an open mind. As with the vignette, an attempt is made to do justice to the ambiguity of experiences in the reading of the anecdote and not to define them conclusively (see Peterlini, Cennamo and Donlic 2020: 119).

The potential of anecdotes for experience-orientated research

Anecdotes bring to light experiences that conversation partners recount from their memories, how they reflect on their experiences and how they evaluate them from today's point of view. The texts convey both the expressive and the inexpressive, allowing readers to trace experiences in a way that is difficult to do in any other form. In contrast to excerpts from interviews or conversations, these short narrative texts with the quality of the *punctum* often succeed in condensing remembered experiences in such a way that excesses are created, that an atmosphere, moods and pathological events can be (co-)experienced. By making remembered experiences comprehensible in anecdotes, readers' (implicit) prior knowledge and experiences are thematized and possibly provoked. In this way, readers can co-experience the experiences narrated in the anecdote (Meyer-Drawe 2012a) and generate new insights. Bodily aspects of expression and experience contribute to creating the anecdote and enriching it with a surplus of insight through resonance reading: 'Sensual-bodily perception and its pathic structure are fundamental for the generation of productive perspectives on the new and unknown as well as the creative evocation of new meaning beyond a reconstruction of already existing general meaning' (Agostini 2020: 169).

Notes

1 The research centres of phenomenological vignette and anecdote research have joined forces in the VignA network: https://vigna.univie.ac.at/.

2 That people can co-experience the experiences of others is a crucial theoretical and methodological assumption of vignette and anecdotal research; see the explanation in the section 'Co-experience in the perspective of body and responsivity' in Chapter 3.
3 *Oxford English Dictionary*: https://www.oed.com/viewdictionaryentry/Entry/7367. Accessed 12 July 2023, Anecdote.
4 'Anekdote', in: *Deutsches Wörterbuch von Jacob Grimm und Wilhelm Grimm, Neubearbeitung (1965–2018)*, digitized version in *Digitales Wörterbuch der deutschen Sprache*, https://www.dwds.de/wb/dwb2/anekdote. Accessed 7 January 2023.
5 The hyphen between *merk* and *würdig* highlights the double meaning of the German term *merkwürdig*, which in common usage stands for strange, but when interpreted literally, also means 'worthy of being remembered'.

CHAPTER 2

History and positioning to similar approaches

Chapter 2 presents the history of ideas and the epistemological foundations of the methodology, situating anecdote research in a historical context while highlighting more recent innovations and distinguishing them from earlier strands. In a further section, we position anecdote research in its relationship to related research approaches, discussing similarities and differences.

2.1 Origin and conceptual development

Between 2009 and 2013, two research projects funded by the Austrian Science Fund (FWF) were carried out at the University of Innsbruck under the title 'Personal Education Processes in Heterogeneous Groups'. They aimed to investigate phenomena of learning as they occur in the personal learning processes of pupils in heterogeneous groups in the first year of learning at various new secondary school locations throughout Austria.[1] Based on the co-experience with pupils in their everyday school life, vignettes that 'linguistically condense selected moments of lived school experience' were created (ibid.: 33).

In the project's second phase,[2] the interviews and surveys focused on the pupils' experiences over the first four years of secondary school. In addition, the interviews also focused on the pupils' future prospects in light of their imminent completion of lower secondary school. As the pupils were in their eighth year and would be leaving school afterwards, the research team was particularly interested in what school experiences they remembered most in retrospect. For fourteen-year-olds in Austria, leaving the middle school is a decisive step in their future lives, as they are about to transition to upper secondary school, an apprenticeship or a career. School reports play a significant role when it comes to educational pathways. However, little consideration is given to the formative learning and school experiences that determine young people's relationships with themselves, others and the world (see Rathgeb, Krenn and Schratz 2017).

The starting point and motive for the search for a further research method during the second phase of the research project was the desire not only to record the shared experience *in media res* in the form of vignettes but also to depict educational processes over time. In addition, the fact that the pupils – then in the first year of the new secondary school – met with the researchers in the eighth grade as thirteen- and fourteen-year-olds prompted the participants in the research group to include the interview transcripts, that is, the statements, stories and reflections of the young people about their memories of their secondary school years, more closely in the investigations. To do justice to these concerns, the researchers were initially inspired by the *anecdote* repeatedly used by Max van Manen (1990; 1997) in his studies but subsequently broke new ground.

In the definition of the proposed research approach, an anecdote is a memorable and noteworthy (*merk-würdig*) story which pointedly condenses events from the recalled experience of an interviewee with particular impact (cf. Rathgeb, Krenn and Schratz 2017: 130). In addition, the characteristics of *a topic, a focus, an experience and a punchline* were recorded for the anecdote.

Further differentiations of the research method were made in writing, revising and enriching the texts in the group. Above all, there was agreement that writing anecdotes – similar to writing vignettes (Agostini, Eloff and Schratz 2024) – is not about depicting the narrated experiences in detail but about condensing the affecting (memorable, peculiar, pleasing, disturbing, curious) aspects of a particular moment in a way that captures the complexity, richness and liveliness of such experiences as closely as possible. The anecdote should not be *cleansed* of the experience of the conversation shared by the researcher and the researched, but rather, this should further inspire the writing process. Non-verbal and bodily aspects like the manner of speaking and silence, hesitation, whispering, faltering, stammering and talking loudly or quietly are essential elements of the texts. Bodily expressions bear the potential to resonate with the recalled experience in the anecdote.

Vignettes and anecdotes share the aim of tracing the lived experiences of pupils. However, anecdotes do not narrate experiences captured *in media res* but rather recalled and narrated experiences. Consequently, other new aspects, in particular those of remembering and forgetting and the linguistic expression of these remembered experiences, play a central role in the conception of this text type, and an examination of these is essential for the theoretical foundation of the anecdote (see Chapter 3). The basis of writing anecdotes is the transcripts of conversations, which places their qualities, conception and realization at the centre of attention (see Chapter 4).

The history of the anecdote began in the school context. However, the method has spread in various educational and social fields, both as a research tool and as a basis for practical reflection in the professional development of specialists or organizational development. Anecdote research can be combined well with other research methods, such as vignette research or ethnographic methods that describe lifeworlds (e.g. photo voice, interview walk), in research projects with mixed method designs. A combination with quantitative methods is also conceivable (see Chapter 7).

2.2 Related research approaches

Like other research approaches and methodologies, anecdote research did not emerge in a vacuum. It is related to and inspired by other approaches and methods of experience-orientated lifeworld research. This section presents related research approaches, defining similarities and differences to phenomenological anecdote research.

Vignette research

Not least because anecdote research developed from the same research project, it is closest to phenomenological vignette research (Agostini, Eloff and Schratz 2024). There are many similarities between the two research methods, but there are also differences: like the vignette, the anecdote is a literary but non-fictional type of text. Like the vignette, it is a 'short, concise narrative' (Schratz, Schwarz and Westfall-Greiter 2012: 34), which captures 'moments of lived (learning) experiences … in narrative form' (ibid.: 31).

Similar to vignettes, anecdotes are understood as an *event in sound* – in this case, however, of remembered experiences (see Henriksson and Saevi 2009); anecdotes should also be *concise* in the sense of pregnant, substantial and expressive with regard to the lived experience.

Like the vignette, an anecdote should enable readers to have an experience in the sense of co-experience; like the vignette, the anecdote is not intended to *instruct* but to enthral (see Meyer-Drawe 2012a: 15). This is made possible above all by the fact that the pathic finds its way into the anecdote, that excess that characterizes not only remembering and storytelling but every question-and-answer event.

The proximity to the *example* that Meyer-Drawe attributes to the vignette (2012a: 13) is also essential for the anecdote. By this, the anecdote also shows a 'tendency towards the concrete' (ibid.), eludes definition and does not subordinate itself to a general; instead, the 'specifically general' only becomes recognizable 'in the passage through it' (ibid.). However, the example does not serve to reconstruct the individual case, as would be evident in casuistry, but rather an understanding of general contexts in the respective case (see Agostini 2020).

The essential difference between a vignette and an anecdote is that the vignette is restricted to the description of co-experienced situations. In contrast, the anecdote represents a method for conducting and interpreting interviews and conversations by including descriptions of the conversational situation and bodily expressions while speaking. The vignette thus aims at lived experiences in *statu nascendi*, whereas the anecdote focuses on remembered experiences that are actualized in a conversation.

Consequently, co-experience is also vital when writing the anecdotes; researchers adopt a co-experiential attitude in the conversation or interview situation, and this participation in the *experiences of others* flows into the texts, just as it does when writing vignettes.

Anecdotes in the work of Max van Manen

Van Manen anecdotes are mainly based on observations ('closely observing situations'). This approach is similar to the writing of vignettes, in which, however, the focus is not on co-experience through perception but on the most direct possible description of personal experiences, either from personal experience or from interviews (see van Manen 1990: 69). According to Max van Manen, anecdotes can also be written in the first person from the perspective of the person recounting their own experience. An example:

Anecdote 3

As I make my morning coffee, I look out of the kitchen window. I see a hummingbird land on the feeder and I smile. And yet, I do not pay much attention. I am kind of sunken in thought as I stare out of the window. I know I have to do a bunch of jobs today but cannot bring myself to focus on them either. I wonder what my kids were doing last night. The morning seems to be slipping by and I have the vague feeling that I should be accomplishing more with regards to the things that matter. 'A penny for your thoughts', I hear my wife say. She has torn me away from my dreamy staring out of the window. 'What were you thinking?' she asks. (I don't usually like questions like that. I don't even honestly know what to say about my state of mind). 'Oh, nothing really', I respond. But my wife keeps pressing, 'You looked so intent!' 'Well, I was admiring the orchids in the kitchen window sill', I respond. 'It is amazing how they keep blooming week after week.' My wife, the gardener, seems pleased with my explanation, though I can see from her face that she expected something else. (van Manen 2016: 31)

Max van Manen's merit lies above all in the scholarly rehabilitation of the anecdote through his profound theoretical work.

Methodologically, no strict guidelines for anecdotes can be recognized. His openness to the sources of the content condensed in the anecdotes inevitably also opens up freedoms in form and presentation by his conviction 'that the method of phenomenology is that there is no method' (van Manen 1997: 30).

Anecdotes in the work of Hans Blumenberg

Alongside metaphorology and mythology, the anecdote is one of the three elements of Hans Blumenberg's *theory of non-conceptuality* (see Zill 2014: 26). According to Blumenberg, anecdotes are short stories whose protagonists are well-known personalities characterized by true or invented stories or sayings (ibid.). There is a proximity to Arrighetti's (2007) analysis of the anecdote in ancient texts or to the understanding of Nietzsche, who believed that it was possible to draw a picture of a person based on three anecdotes ([1873] 1973: 297). In addition, Blumenberg also processes excerpts from letters or diaries into anecdotes or writes 'imaginary anecdotes' (Zill 2014: 27), which serve to vividly illustrate 'a meaning – for example, that of a philosophical system'. For instance, in his volume *Der Prozess der theoretischen Neugierde* (*The Process of Theoretical Curiosity*) (1988), Blumenberg presents the characteristics of epochs and their central ideas pictorially using anecdotes. It is instructive to note that Blumenberg's anecdotes do not exist independently of their use in concrete texts, that is, reflecting on the texts forms the indispensable context (ibid.: 33). This brief description clearly shows that the anecdote has an entirely different function in Blumenberg's philosophical thought than the textual form presented in this volume, which is used primarily as a research instrument.

Collective memory work with Frigga Haug

The German sociologist and psychologist Frigga Haug developed memory work in the early 1970s – together with a group of socialist women – as a social science research method that saw itself as an 'emancipatory learning project' (1999: 227) aiming for liberation. *Collective memory work* was also met with a great response internationally, with adaptations and variations also emerging (Hyle et al. 2008; Hamm 2020; 2021). In contrast to anecdote research, in the concept of Haug, the participants themselves wrote down their remembered experiences, which were analysed collectively. Similarities with anecdote research include the focus on experience, the importance of working in groups and the reference to recording *an* experience, *an* event or *a* scene (Haug 1999: 203).

Biographical and narrative research

Biographical research uses life-history narratives in oral or textual form as a basis for generating knowledge about life trajectories. When analysing the data, the focus is, on the one hand, on reconstructing individual biographies and, on the other hand, on the social conditions that influence these life courses and designs. Narrative research not only 'looks at the conditions, characteristics, intentions, contexts of use and lines of development of narrative' (Fuchs 2011: 125) but also analyses life–history narratives. While the context of the conversation is essential in anecdote research and flows into the texts, this aspect plays a lesser role in biographical and narrative research. Another difference is that while anecdotes are based on data obtained through interviews or conversations, they are written in a retelling manner by the researchers – taking into account the shared experience in the conversation. Biographical and narrative research, on the other hand, are based exclusively on primary sources, that is, audio recordings of stories, interview transcripts, diary excerpts and the like. The research questions and concerns in anecdote research are not predetermined, so the interpretation or reading of the texts can be approached from very different perspectives (see Chapter 6).

Compost writing by Donna Haraway

Haraway (2019) speaks of *compost narratives* as an alternative to autobiographical writing, which for her is an expression of the illusion 'of self-telling and self-forming'. The philosopher justifies compost writing by stating that 'nothing makes itself, nothing tells its own story' (ibid.: 565). In her work, personal stories, *earth stories* or invented stories ('author's science fiction stories') can help to emphasize collective togetherness and strengthen the problematic search for cross-species reproductive justice. Haraway points out that who tells which stories about whom and who can tell his or her story at all is crucial. In stories, structures of colonization and power are established or also transgressed and disrupted. Haraway points out that 'compost stories live in the wake of history, never clean and original, always for some worlds and not others' (ibid.: 573). Although many of Haraway's considerations can be fruitful for anecdote research, the differences between the two approaches are apparent.

Notes

1 This is the fifth grade as the entry year into the trial phase of the reform model '*Neue Mittelschule*', which was introduced in the 2008–9 school year to replace the former *Hauptschule*.
2 The FWF (Austrian Science Fund) funded the second project phase under the number P 225373-G16.

CHAPTER 3

Theoretical foundations and implications for practice

3.1 'Back to the things themselves'

'Phenomenological research is the study of lived experience', as van Manen (1990: 9) summed up Husserl's philosophy: 'To say the same differently: phenomenology is the study of the lifeworld – the world as we immediately experience it pre-reflectively rather than as we conceptualize, categorize, or reflect on it'. How does this reconcile with research that uses anecdotes obtained from conversations as its main tool? The experiences condensed in the anecdotes did not occur instantly but are often recalled with a significant time lag and have often already been reflected upon by the individuals involved. Moreover, anecdotes are not primarily descriptive texts like, for example, the vignettes from the same research approach. Rather, they combine descriptive moments with spoken narration in a linguistic art form.

To provide an epistemological foundation for anecdote research, it is necessary to outline some basic assumptions of phenomenology, even if this is only possible here in a selective and simplified manner. Husserl's imperative to 'go back to the things themselves' (Husserl [1900–1] 2001a: 168) first and foremost does not address the things themselves but rather the 'openness to the world' of research as a 'participation that we call experience' (Steinbock 1997: 127).

This participation and entanglement of researchers with the things they explore represents – if understood as a method and research attitude – a first prerequisite for a direct engagement with the world and its things. For Merleau-Ponty ([1945] 2005: vii), phenomenology requires 're-achieving a direct and primitive contact with the world ... to give a direct description of our experience as it is, without taking into account its psychological origin and the causal explanations which the scientist, the historian or the sociologist may be able to provide'. The most crucial effort towards a phenomenological research approach is the step back from assuming sure and reconstructive knowledge that can tell us how things *are*. With the Ancient Greek term ἐποχή (*epoché*), Edmund Husserl means 'to hold back' or 'to withhold' judgement about the essence or facticity of a thing, referring back to the philosophical school of the Stoa (Husserl [1913] 2014: 31). It may be admitted that one can never wholly free oneself from preconceptions and prior experiences because these not only guide and limit understanding but also enable it in the first place. However, the validity of preconceptions is withdrawn through 'eidetic reduction' (see Rother 2002), in that they are to a certain extent 'overridden' or 'bracketed' in the sense of epoché (Husserl [1913] 2014: 55). This allows us to attempt to gain a clearer view of the phenomena as they present themselves to the senses.

Thus, Husserl is not concerned with the factual explanation of a thing but with exploring the 'manifold of all possible perceptual exhibitings' of an object or thing (Husserl [1936] 1970: 162). It is not merely a matter of describing what a thing essentially *is*, but rather how it *appears* in our perception – following the meaning of *phenomenon* in Latin and Ancient Greek as 'thing appearing to view', based on *phainein* for 'to shine through' or 'to show' (Stevenson 2010: 1334). To be accessible to phenomenological observation, a thing in Husserl's sense does not necessarily have to be concrete and tangible: 'Anything that presents itself to consciousness is potentially of interest to phenomenology, whether the object is real or imagined, empirically measurable or subjectively felt' (van Manen 1990: 9). To investigate the phenomenon of angels, for example, it is not necessary to prove that angels exist. The aim of the phenomenological investigation will not be to verify or falsify the existence of angels but rather their appearance in human consciousness or conceptions. The range goes from exploring the diversity of representations of angels in different places of worship of different religions in different epochs to examining how angelic apparitions appear in human dreams or are allegorized in literary artefacts. The result of such an enquiry will be a – not limitlessly possible – unfolding of the manifold appearances of angels in human visions and descriptions to better understand the phenomenon of angels.

Describing – crucial for legitimating anecdotes phenomenologically – means more than 'the mere depiction of matters of or even an expression of one's own inner feeling states' (Steinbock 1997: 127). Steinbock thus refers to two problems of phenomenological research. One problem is reducing phenomenological research to a pure introspection or 'phenomenological autobiography' (ibid.: 128). As valuable as it can be to start from one's own experiences, it would be limiting to leave it at that and to forego intersubjectively viable statements. The other danger would be to misunderstand phenomenology as factual research. Phenomenology moves in a creative tension between a thoroughly rigorous scholarly attitude and trust in intuitive understanding, summarized by Merleau-Ponty in the concept of '"intellectual intuition", which is not an occult faculty, but perception itself before it is reduced to ideas, perception dormant within itself, in which all things are me because I am not yet the subject of reflection' (Merleau-Ponty 1970: 75). Merleau-Ponty thus emphasizes both the connection between the researcher and the object they want to understand and the prioritization of knowledge over its classification into categories. In his working notes in *The Visible and the Invisible* (Merleau-Ponty [1964] 1968), he justifies this self-contained perception of the world from the body, which we do not have, but with which we are in the world and through which we are interwoven with the world so that we cannot have the distance of an autonomously reflecting subject towards it. Cognition becomes possible through 'perceiving-perceived *Einfühlung*' (248, emphasis on the German word *Einfühlung* for intuition, sensitivity, empathy in the original). According to Merleau-Ponty, such 'knowing by sentiment' takes place 'between it and us' (ibid.: 249). In this context, Hermann Schmitz's New Phenomenology also offers valuable approaches, as it aims 'to make their actual lives comprehensible to humans', explicitly including 'spontaneous life experience' (Schmitz 2019: 43). For Schmitz, too, access to spontaneous life experience is not Descartes' cogito but the lived body, which Schmitz also calls the felt body and which he locates between understanding and involvement (Griffero 2019: 11).

The fact that cognition occurs *between* a thing and an observer addresses another vital issue of phenomenological epistemology. How the world and its appearance in human perception are connected has been the subject of complex and ultimately unresolved debates, from Husserl to contemporary phenomenology (see Crowell 2023). For phenomenological epistemology, however, it is mainly beyond doubt that there is a connection between perception and reality. Accordingly, aspects (*shades*) of an actually existing reality are revealed in perceptions, not as the Kantian 'thing itself' but rather in the sense of a 'demand-character' or 'invitation-character', which is inherent to things in relation to human perception and to which this consciousness is 'intentional' (directed) (see Bengtsson 2002: 525).

The subjectivity of anecdotes, criticizable at first glance, appears in a different light against this theoretical background. Anecdotes do not assert an absolute reality. However, they bring out aspects of it in an exemplary manner, which also achieve intersubjective character and general significance through a twofold cognitive process. On the one hand, anecdotes arise from people's memories of previous experiences in a current conversational situation. The extent to which these remembered experiences correspond to a factual truth can be bracketed in the sense of *epoché* and eidetic reduction since phenomenology is not concerned with reconstructing a verifiable reality. For example, in an interview or conversation, Mr or Ms X talks about unfair treatment in childhood that still hurts them today. It would probably be difficult, if not impossible, to determine whether this injustice occurred exactly as person X tells it. One would have to undertake biographical or historical research, interview X's environment at the time, and ask parents, classmates, teachers, neighbours and, of course, the accused persons. We can assume that no sure result will emerge but that new doubts and questions will arise – in the sense of the hermeneutic circle, which does not promise a reliable final result but rather a partial and gradual approximation to reality, without ever reaching it definitively with 100 per cent certainty. According to the phenomenological perspective, however, the question of historical truth is bracketed. The aim is not to prove or disprove the truth of the narrated fact but to learn something about general issues from X's remembered experience. Such insights could be, for example, the connection between X's interpretation of unfair treatment in light of their idea of justice. Even if X had remembered the unjust treatment one-sidedly or ultimately wrongly, this connection between a remembered experience and developing a sense of justice would be an exciting phenomenon worth reflecting on. Another example is the following anecdote, discussed once more in another chapter as an application example. Here, we will question it for its insight value, independent of the truth.

Anecdote 4

'I had five fives',[1] Ahmed[2] answers when asked about his school report from the fourth grade of middle school.[3] 'Because of exams', he explains the situation. He now wants to study even more for his exams, as he can do more than the grades show. 'I can do better ...' he falters momentarily, swallowing the last syllable. He starts again, smiling cautiously: 'I can ... do better at ... studying.' He falls silent, and his smile fades, then he murmurs: 'And I can only get better in exams.' In a firmer voice, he adds: 'I always get fives on exams, but I do study. He emphasizes the word 'but', sighs, and quietly, almost tonelessly, he adds: 'I don't know why either.' (Peterlini et al. 2021: 117)

Ahmed recounts his negative experiences with school grades. The extent to which his fives are justified is simply not verifiable in a phenomenological investigation. It has to be bracketed. However, it is interesting and epistemologically sound to consider the difficulty of understanding his failing grades that emerge in the reminiscent conversation. This passage shows how a remembered experience can become a lived experience in conversation. Ahmed's insecurity, his helplessness, appears directly in the conversation and, in addition to the reproduction of what was said, also flows into the anecdote when it describes how he emphasizes the word 'but' – perceivable in his voice – then sighs and eventually becomes quieter, almost to the point of falling silent. Even if we were dealing with the best and fairest teacher in the world and Ahmed was an absolutely lazy pupil, the anecdote shows – with quite general significance – the discrepancy between a mathematical assessment system and the efforts and self-assessments of a pupil.

Husserl's 'thing itself' reveals its phenomenological significance for research practice in these examples, albeit in a simplification of the complexity of philosophical-phenomenological epistemology, as Langefeld (1972: 105; van Manen and van Manen, 2021a: 1077), for example, considers unavoidable for doing phenomenology versus thinking phenomenology. Anecdotes cannot fathom or even assert factual truth. In the case of anecdotes, the 'thing itself' is nothing other than that which forces its way from memory into the reproduction of the speaker in a current conversational situation and thus becomes present.

A second moment of academic validation is fundamental in phenomenology: the spoken word is expressed verbally and non-verbally, that is, bodily, in the attentive presence of at least one other person. The anecdote is primarily created in this transition of the spoken memory of one person to the perception and consequently to the consciousness of another. If the person speaking allows themselves to be guided by the flow of their memories and their realized dismay, it is up to the listener to allow themselves to be 'called' and 'affected' by it. It could well be that the person speaking – driven by memories as ongoing lived experiences – misses the meaning of what is said, just as they cannot be aware of their body language because it is challenging to observe themselves simultaneously when speaking and acting, whether they are sighing, lowering or raising their voice. To paraphrase Husserl, the interaction between the 'demand-characters' or 'invitation-characters' of the spoken word and the other person's intentional (directed) attention occurs at the moment of the emerging anecdote.

In this context, consciousness in the phenomenological sense must not be understood as a distanced human access to things, as could still be the case to some extent with Husserl – despite his realization of this impossibility. The concept of the body, which Merleau-Ponty coined based on Husserl, also plays a central role in epistemology. For Merleau-Ponty, human existence takes place not so much in or with a body but directly *as* a body: 'I am my body' ([1945] 2005: 231). This famous sentence applies to the idea of consciousness not as a rational or spiritual counterpart to a material world but as interwoven with that world. Thus, the recognizing subject cannot have an external view of the world, as Meyer-Drawe concludes in her discussion of Merleau-Ponty's critique of Husserl: 'Corporeality remains a provocation of the architecture of cognition; it sabotages the sorting into subject and object, into inside and outside, into active and passive, because it is always on both sides of the event' (Meyer-Drawe 1996: 213). Therefore, when we speak of phenomena as appearances in consciousness, we are not talking about a consciousness, which is separate from things and able to grasp them completely: 'The body undermines the privilege of the ego as the centre of the creation of meaning' (ibid.: 214). Instead, it is a matter of using phenomenological research to 'grasp the entanglement of the recognising ego with the world and thus to regain an amazement that marks its possibilities precisely in the perspective of the limits of our knowledge' (ibid.: 202). For anecdote research, the phenomena emerge from multiple entanglements: of the narrating I with the world in its past and present, between this I and the conversational situation, between the I and the listening Other, who in turn is entangled with their own experiences, their presuppositions, with the conversational situation and with the interlocutor.

3.2 Recalled experiences

Memory as a starting point for academic knowledge is a question of varied, sometimes contentious discourses. The focus is traditionally on psychological and, currently, mainly neuroscientific approaches, which, in addition to allocating memory to some regions of the brain, primarily investigate questions of the reliability and manipulability of memory (cf. Slotnick 2012). For qualitative research, memories are sometimes indispensable approaches, that is, for questions of contemporary history, generational research, cultural analysis and social research, personal and collective identity formation, biographical and educational research and myth research.

In such a wide-open perspective, memory becomes – in modification of the definition by John Locke as a 'storehouse of our ideas' – a 'storehouse whose stores are nothing stored nowhere'. With this wordplay, David Farell Krell (1982: 492) explains the difficulty of grasping memory empirically in his essay on the 'Phenomenology of Memory'. Husserl's examination of the scholarly evidence surrounding memory is correspondingly complex throughout his life's work. Regardless of the partly intricate and repeatedly revised intellectual attempts, 'Husserl's approach takes memory to be a source of *phenomenological evidence*' (ibid.: 493; emphasis in the original).

Retrospective understanding is an indispensable endeavour for phenomenology, on which it is also dependent in its interest in what is presently given and happening. Lived experience, as the central object of research in phenomenology, can only ever be grasped retrospectively. Consequently, we need to understand how experience, which permanently disappears into the past, can be brought back into the present through contemplation and reflection. For Husserl, experience takes place in a flowing continuum that we must literally swim along without ever being able to capture entirely and comprehensively (Husserl [1913] 2014: 79). 'It is essentially a flow that we can swim after, starting from the present moment, when we fix our focus reflectively on it, while the stretches lying further back are lost for perception. Only in the form of retention or in the form of recollection looking back do we have a consciousness of what has immediately come to a close' (ibid.).

Husserl uses the concept of retention to explain why we can, for example, hear a melody even though we are actually dealing with individual tones flowing along in rapid succession. Human memory enables us to hold back the sound that has just reached our ears until the next present sound arrives, with which the remembered sound is associated. This recourse to memory interacts with an anticipatory expectation, which Husserl calls *protention* or *anticipation*. In this interplay of past, present and future, the musical theme emerges as a composition of reception. With this example, Husserl demonstrates how we constantly move in a 'stream of experience' (ibid.: 80). To fully comprehend the unity of this stream tangibly, in Husserl's words, an 'apprehension that swims along with it completely, is intrinsically impossible'. Rather it is facilitated in the case of already-known melodies.

However, this theory of remembering raises a problem that phenomenology shares with Gestalt psychology (Albertazzi 1999). The fact that previous experiences are sedimented in our (also bodily) consciousness has the advantage that we can quickly categorize repetitive or similar events into a familiar overall picture. For example, we inevitably recognize a stick figure in a particular arrangement of lines with a circle on top, even if the individual lines are not connected but separated by a gap. By recalling the memorized figure, the consciousness fills in the gaps to form a complete figure. A specific arrangement of black spots on a white background will allow us to recognize a Dalmatian, although here, too, the spots are not connected at all. Here, too, the reception will complete the shape from the memory of the shape of a dog. Like music, the conscious mind assembles the separate individual parts into a figuration in the memory and confirms the anticipated expectations. This way, we can quickly categorize things into existing patterns, forms and explanatory models and find our way around (Luccio 1999: 131). The downside of this remarkable ability is that we also need help to abandon familiar patterns of perception and categorization or withdraw from their suggestive power to obtain a foreign or second view. Sedimented experiences have a great power over us: 'The world is to us what we perceive, but we need to re-learn to perceive because we are accustomed to taking for perceived what we *think* we have perceived' (Meyer-Drawe 1996: 199).

As can be seen from these geometric figures (Figures 1 and 2), we also tend to insert deviations into the orders stored in our memory by manipulating them. Thus, where observers look at these representations, they usually see a circle and a square; even though the circle is not complete and the square is missing an edge.

The same happens to us with lines, however incomplete and awkward, if they could be the outline of a face (Figure 3). And once we have recognized a face in these lines, we can hardly see anything other than the face, even if these lines are now part of a completely different, irregular form (Figure 4). Whether we want to or not, we see the face, even though it may only be an irregular shape. We can usually read words that we know even if only the first and last letters are in place and all the others are randomly swapped (Figure 5).

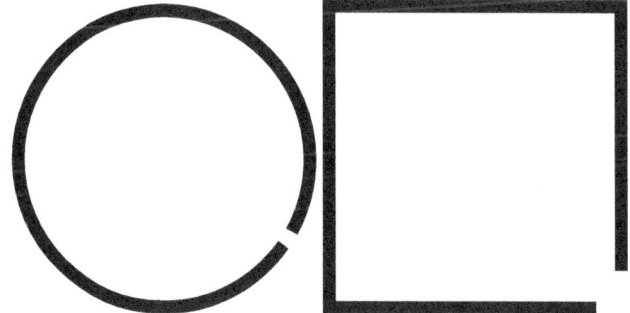

FIGURES 1 AND 2 *The completion of known shapes.*

FIGURES 3 AND 4 *Irregular lines or something we know?*

PRCEPEIOTN

FIGURE 5 *Can you read it?*

These examples, which seem simple, are of far-reaching significance for the phenomenological research approach. If, for example, teachers, social workers or managers in organizations have stored a particular image of humanity, they will tend to organize the people entrusted to them – children, young people, people in need, employees – into this existing mental framework. The more ingrained their expectations are and the less open they are to experiencing them fully, the easier it will be for them to overlook possibilities or problems on this side of categorical prejudices. By consciously pausing before each judgement, the phenomenological exercise consists of hampering the convenient but often misleading and reductive shortcut of classifying people, situations and contexts. In this way, space is opened to the perception of the *matter itself* before categorizing it according to predetermined world and value systems. Wolfgang Köhler provided essential contributions to a phenomenological understanding of memory in Gestalt psychology. He criticized introspective psychology, which ignored internal-external connections, and also behaviourism, which focuses exclusively on external behaviour. Instead, he shifted academic interest to the pre-categorical 'insight or immediate intuition of dependency relationships ... which determines behaviour even before the mind becomes aware of the structure of a situation' (Bozzi 1999: 44). Such an approach coincides with the phenomenological claim of interrupting or at least delaying the categorizing classification into existing patterns of order. Fixed ideological and metaphysical prejudices are replaced by the analysis 'of the field of experience in terms of expressiveness: tone of voice, facial or gestural mimicry, the environmental and cognitive context, together constitute the phenomenological conditions of the act of comprehension' (ibid.). In this view, memory is also 'based on the understanding of relationships' (ibid.).

The external 'curse' that drives past events into internalization is one of the central motifs of Freud's psychoanalysis. He developed less a theory of memory than one of forgetting. However, through the dynamics of repression and splitting off of lived experience, it offers a plausible explanatory model for how memory is suppressed or distorted and can be painstakingly brought up and liberated through psychoanalysis. Traumatic events that the individual cannot cope with are repressed. This psychodynamic also concerns embarrassing experiences and actions for the individual, that is, tainted with shame and guilt, because they contrast with internalized social norms or beliefs. From a phenomenological perspective, this raises the question of how the phenomenon of forgetting is related to memory and how forgetting and remembering co-determine what of past experiences 'appears in the living present' (Hopkins 2023: 102).

Individual memory is socially conditioned and, in turn, constructs social memory. Maurice Halbwachs's groundbreaking theory of collective memory shows how his supposedly highly personal memory of a walk in a foreign city is influenced by a number of factors, including what someone had previously told him about this city, what he had read in the descriptions of the town, as well as what he knew about influenced perception, exemplified by him standing on a bridge and acknowledging the effect of that specific perspective. Even Charles Dickens appears as his invisible companion because a passage from one of the writer's novels occurred to him while he was out walking (Halbwachs 1967: 2–3). The memory of childhood events is therefore also influenced by the values that were important at the time, what was publicly appreciated and what was taboo, how parents viewed the same events and how siblings reacted to them. Continuing Halbwachs's theory, Jan Assmann distinguishes four external dimensions of individual memory, namely:

1. the mimetic memory: it affects everything we do, from cookbooks to building instructions;
2. the memory of things: bed, chair, eating and washing utensils, clothes, tools, houses, villages, roads, vehicles, ships;
3. communicative memory: language, exchange with others;
4. cultural memory: 'transmission of meaning', that is, the mimetic routine can become a rite and acquire meaning, thus going beyond the memory of the action (J. Assmann 2002: 19; J. Assmann 2011).

According to Jan Assmann, collective memories also determine the individual's memory (36). How people remember historical events thus also depends on textbooks, monuments, songs and stories, and in a broader sense, political frameworks, structural conditions (school, social system and power relations), religious and ideological orientations. From this perspective, the scholarly approach to memory does not necessarily focus on the question of truth but instead on examining the conditions that influence remembering from the past and how and what significance this has for the present. In further developing Jan Assmann's theory, Aleida Assmann (2015) has thus created a concept of social and dialogic memory that shows how the negotiation of memory content in the present can contribute to change processes. Similarly, Merleau-Ponty recognizes from a phenomenological perspective how psychoanalysis has also developed from a fact-oriented analysis of the past to the use of memory for present-oriented and future-oriented healing processes:

> Freud's contribution is not to have revealed quite another reality beneath appearances but that the analysis of given behaviour always discovers several layers of signification, each with its own truth, and that the plurality of possible interpretations is the discursive expression of a mixed life in which every choice

always has several meanings, it being impossible to say which of them is the only true one. (Merleau-Ponty 1970: 50)

Whether the experience of an injury from childhood is truthfully reproduced is less critical for the treatment than the question of what meaning a person gives to their memory and what understandings and creative possibilities open up to them in the narrative.

Here is an example of an anecdote in which the stories from a focus group discussion with the pupils Kerim and Karl flow together:

Anecdote 5

> Ms Krumm, the former English teacher, was walking past the class when a pencil flew into her face through the open door, the pupils say. The door was open, and Karl had thrown the pen outside during an argument. 'And then right in her eye', Kerim sighs. And then Ms Krumm was crying. She shouted at the class and said that she felt threatened. 'You need to put a tea bag on your eye', Karl recommended. However, Ms Krumm was just going through the motions. Karl points a finger at his forehead, indicating that she was acting crazy. Kerim replies: 'But it didn't actually hit her, it grazed her or something. Kerim is convinced that Ms Krumm was acting. 'It was just the shock', Karl replies sympathetically. The teacher then left the school. (Ammann et al. 2017: 189)

This anecdote is based on a focus group discussion with students in an eighth-grade class at an Austrian middle school. Half of the students participating in the interview have Turkish or Serbo-Croatian as their first language. The story emerges from the joint recollection and verbalization of the participants in the discussion.

Kerim initially describes the very problematic scene with certainty that the pen thrown by Karl hit the teacher 'right in her eye'. Nevertheless, he qualifies this by saying the pencil did not 'actually' hit her but 'grazed her or something'. Although it should be a relevant question for the boys whether the teacher was hit or not, the dramatic event in the anecdote is not fully explained. It is not the aim or intention of anecdote research to prove the factual truth. Instead, the anecdote reveals subtle clues as to how the pupils re-experience the unfortunate event in their memories and how they deal with it in the present. Kerim 'sighs' as he describes the incident. This bodily expression refers to regret and to being affected. Verbally, however, he plays down the incident and even insinuates that the teacher was just putting on an act. From there, readers could consider whether the subsequent bodily dismay gives way on a cognitive level to a defence against guilt by trivializing the incident and blaming the victim. Karl, the involuntary perpetrator, in turn, concedes to the teacher that she was shocked. In doing so, he conciliatingly excuses her rude behaviour when she responds to his good advice to put a tea bag on her eye by making a sign with her finger calling him crazy. There is no lack of ambiguity in the anecdote, but it offers a wide range of possible interpretations for dealing with an unfortunate event, ranging from consternation, minimizing guilt, insulting the victim and reconciling with the memory.

Between attempting to attribute evidence to memories and realizing their fragility, Husserl's theory of memory is also not free of uncertainties and contradictions. He does ask himself the question 'whether reproductive consciousness is trustworthy' (Krell 1982: 495). He distinguishes fresh retention as primary memory from reproductive recollection as secondary, starting from the now-point of perceptual experience. While in retention, the moment that has just passed can still be recorded reasonably reliably, 'to recall the distant past is more problematic' (ibid.: 501). The assumption of the reliability of memory contrasts with the basic phenomenological assumptions that it is not the Kantian thing in itself that appears in consciousness but rather shadows of a manifold and, therefore, never fully graspable reality. The modes of appearance are subject to the 'law of modification' (Hopkins 2023: 102) and are subject to discontinuities, 'of both the past and that which is forgotten from present consciousness' (ibid.). In an essay on the origin of geometry, Husserl makes a connection between sedimentation and forgetting that is missing in the English translation: 'Sedimentation is always somehow forgetfulness' (Husserl 1939: 212, quoted by Hopkins 2023: 104).

Consequently, remembering experiences would be accompanied by both creative shaping and forgetting, which means that the claim of exactness and completeness of memory is no longer possible. This insight makes it all the more important to research remembered experiences and their significance for the present. The reconstructive path of factual research thus loses importance for phenomenology. Its research desideratum concerns the appearance and, therefore, the significance of experiences for the present.

What is interesting for anecdote research is that through reproductive recollection, as is possible in a conversation in the here and now, a 'visualization' takes place (ibid.: 501), the significance of which does not lie in the correctness of the remembered content but in the meaning that it receives for the person remembering through the visualization in the here and now. The purpose of the anecdote is to trace this meaning based on memories actualized in conversation and to entrust it to reconsideration and reflection in the form of a meaningful story. The aim is not to confirm or falsify the contents of memory, which is problematic in terms of scientific theory anyway. Instead, anecdote research engages with what emerges from the interaction of sedimentation and forgetting in conversations with people in the present to explore something about people and the world in an exemplary way.

3.3 Co-experience in the perspective of body and responsivity

Maurice Merleau-Ponty (1970: 46–52) approaches the question of memory in his *Lectures* at the Collège de France 1952–60 via sleep and the unconscious. He illustrates the connection between the three border areas of consciousness with the dilemma of passivity: 'Whether we are trying to understand how consciousness can sleep, how it can be inspired by a past which it has apparently lost, or finally how it can open up again to that past', this is only possible under the condition of dealing with the ambivalence of activity and passivity (ibid.: 46–7). For Merleau-Ponty, sleep is not simply a state of switched-off wakefulness but an altered perception activity. Thus he understands dreams in a Freudian framework ([1900] 1913) as an expression of the unconscious, not simply as a complete absence of consciousness, like emptiness filled by a foolish unconscious. For Merleau-Ponty, reality and the dreamlike cannot be distinguished 'with the simple distinction between consciousness filled by meaning and consciousness given up to its own void' (Merleau-Ponty 1970: 48). Instead, the two modalities are mutually dependent. Some relationships with people and objects in the waking state have a dreamlike character, 'others are present to us in the way that dreams are, the way myths are, and this is enough to question the cleavage between the real and the imaginary' (ibid).

With this weakening and blurring (Peterlini 2023: 4) of supposedly clear and stable boundaries between wakefulness and sleep, dream and reality, conscious and unconscious, Merleau-Ponty attacks the well-established dichotomous structures of our perception. Questioning whether we are always conscious of our presumable rational actions touches on our understanding of the human being. Are we autonomous subjects who can determine their actions and are therefore not subject to any restrictions except those we impose on ourselves without conditioning? Or are we deterministically predetermined subjects trapped in a cosmic order or other external determinations (Merleau-Ponty 1970: 46–7)? The question is decisive for Merleau-Ponty, as 'every theory of perception runs into this problem' (46). He sees the answer in an interpretation of our perceptual experiences, according to which we have 'to become acquainted with a kind of being over which the subject is not sovereign and yet not enclosed within it' (ibid.). With this double negation as neither nor, phenomenology eludes the pull of dichotomies: 'Neither are we *only* autonomous nor *only* conditioned, neither *only* self-determined nor *only* externally determined. As concrete human beings, we find our ways by responding to the situations in which we are entangled. Our freedom is grounded in this latitude of our responses to foreign claims' (Peterlini 2016: 39). The consequence of this perspective is significant in terms of epistemology and research methodology: 'If neither the one nor the other is assured, it remains and helps to engage with the concrete biographic and situational condition, state of mind and life as well as the learning and education practice of our research subjects' (ibid.). Suppose we reject the prefabricated offers of categories as to how the world, other people or situations are to be understood. In that case, the only option left to us is to engage with the world given to us, with its people and situations, as it presents itself to our sensory perception: 'To look, to listen – not completely without theory, but still by setting theory aside in order to grasp the power of the given with one's hands, to appeal to an intensity that is normally forgotten by science and which requires an altered mode of theory' (Gehring 2011: 31).

A prerequisite for such a claim to research is that we recognize others in their experiences. However, is that even possible? For

Ronald D. Laing, evidence is unfeasible without experience: '*Only* experience is evident. Experience is the *only* evidence' (1967: 18). However, he also addresses the dilemma that we can observe the behaviour of others but not their experience: 'I cannot experience your experience. You cannot experience my experience' (ibid.). Consequently, people would remain blind to each other in the area of experience, which is relevant for any evidence. For Laing, this results in the necessity of a constant endeavour so that we can find access to ourselves, to others and to the world: 'I cannot avoid trying to understand your experience because although I do not experience your experience, which is invisible to me (and non-tasteable, non-touchable, non-smellable and inaudible), yet I experience you *as experiencing*' (ibid.: 19).

Here, we find a bridge of understanding across the gap between our own experience and the experience of others. Vignette and anecdote research must transcend the problem of distance and proximity, which is inherent in *participant observation* (see Spradley 1980). Ton Beekmann (1987) took an important step beyond this when he reflected on his experiences with the three-year-old Sasha, whom he knew well, and came to the realization that he could not describe these using participant *observation* but that it was a matter of 'participant *experience*' (Beekman 1983; 1987). In the methodological clarification of vignette and anecdote research, the term was further developed into '*co-experienced experience*' (Peterlini 2016: 11). The terms participant versus co-experienced experience may not seem very different at first glance, but they emphasize different aspects of a research attitude in their epistemic justification. When little Sasha takes big Ton by the hand to watch fireflies with him outside (Beekman 1987: 11), something happens between them that for a research process annuls any distance; the same is the case when Beekman, while reading a book with children, suddenly feels the hand of a child first on his jacket and finally on his neck (ibid.: 13). By using the term *participant experience*, Beekman wants to express that in these moments he cannot speak of *observing* the children because he is *sharing* an experience with them in which both are participating.

Co-experiencing experience places a slightly different emphasis, making a difference epistemologically and methodologically. According to Laing, we can co-experience others as experiencers. This presumption is not a higher claim to truth but rather a 'reduced assertion of truth' (Peterlini 2016b: 23). It means we do not have direct access to the experiences of others, but whatever we understand about these experiences arises from our own experience of the experience of others. Ultimately, nothing can be reliably said about how another person experienced the same situation. Even if the person is subsequently asked about the co-experienced situation, as was attempted in the first vignette and anecdote research projects (Peterlini 2016c), the difficulty of making reliable statements about the experience of the person involved becomes apparent. For example, a child who conspicuously pressed his hands to his face and body during the lesson could not say anything special about it afterwards. The researcher co-experienced his bodily expression as an expression of tension, but the child was obviously not consciously or reflexively aware of it.

The term *co-experienced experience*, therefore, expresses *how* we co-experience others, *not what* others experience. Our perception of others passes through our own experience and becomes a co-experience. Coming back to Beekman, a *co-experienced experience* is not necessarily a *shared experience*. If, for example, our counterpart falters in an interview or conversation and we experience them as unsettled at that moment, this does not mean that we are also disturbed. We cannot claim that we are part of their experience, but we can claim that we have experienced them as insecure. We take part in the same event and are also affected by it. We experience this situation, but we have no sure knowledge of what the other person is experiencing and cannot claim that we have taken part in their experience. With the concept of *interexperience* (Laing 1967: 19), Laing defines the social dimension of phenomenology as 'the science of my own and others' experience. It is concerned with the relation between my experience of you and your experience of me' (ibid.). However, the experience differs in each case and is co-experienced by the participants from their position and perspective.

In anecdote research, the researchers do not experience what the person has experienced in the past. However, they do experience the other person at the moment of remembering. They sit opposite the person, listen and look. The co-experience of the other person occurs through the perception of what is spoken verbally and bodily. The bodily constitution of the human being is also significant for understanding memory (Krell 1982: 403). For Merleau-Ponty, according to his human existence as a body, memory is not simply

PART II
Doing anecdote research

CHAPTER 4

Starting research with conversations and interviews

This chapter introduces this crucial access to anecdote research step by step in a very concrete way: How should researchers prepare for interviews or situations where interesting impromptu conversations are likely to occur? What attitude should they adopt during the interviews? What should they pay attention to? How do they capture co-experience?

4.1 Preparing the conversation and interview

In their volume *Doing Interviews*, Brinkmann and Kvale (2018) describe contrasting epistemological conceptions of interviews using two metaphors: while 'miners' strive to extract existing knowledge like a 'buried metal' from the interviewees in as pure and unaltered a form as possible, 'interviewer-travellers ... wander through the landscape' and explore it as 'unknown territory or with maps, roaming freely around the territory' (20). The 'interviewer-traveller' accompanies the 'local inhabitants, asks questions and encourages them to tell their own stories of their lived world' (ibid.). The experience of the conversation as a *wandering together* not only brings new insights to the dialogue partners but also has the potential to change the participants (see Section 4.2).

Anecdote researchers belong to this second type, as the explanations in Chapter 3 have already shown. This understanding of interviews impacts the entire research process and influences preparation. In particular, this approach is expressed in the attitude co-experience researchers adopt in the field, especially in interviews. This attitude is closely related to the participatory experience (Beekman 1987) (this will be explored further in Section 4.2).

The process of an interview project in the context of anecdote research is essentially no different from other interview studies:

1. Define the topic, objectives and research questions.
2. Develop a research design:
    i. define procedures and methods,
    ii. consider the time frame,
    iii. search for and select interview partners,
    iv. consider questions and create a question guide,
    v. clarify technical questions: recording mode, transcription, data storage and organization and data anonymization,
    vi. clarify ethical aspects and prepare appropriate documents for the dialogue partners (e.g. planned publications, declaration of consent).
3. Contact the interview partners, conduct preliminary talks, familiarize yourself with the field and build trust, arrange appointments, explain ethical aspects, inform about data protection regulations and make written agreements.
4. Conduct and record the interviews and conversations.
5. Transcribe audio files.
6. Write initial versions of anecdotes based on the transcripts and audio recordings (= data processing).
7. Validate and enrich the texts in a research group, with at least one second researcher (using the audio files and transcripts).
8. Revise anecdotes.
9. Interpret anecdotes: writing readings (= data evaluation).

As in any (interview) study, the first step is to clarify the topic and objectives: what exactly should be researched and with what aim? What approach is appropriate for the purpose? Phenomenological studies primarily investigate real-life experiences, aiming to come as close as possible to these and to describe phenomena precisely. To achieve this, phenomenological researchers constantly develop new methods and procedures of description, reduction and variation (Brinkmann 2020: 9).

Not every research question is suitable for phenomenological approaches. Van Manen declares two conditions indispensable for phenomenological analysis: 'an appropriate phenomenological question' and 'experiential material upon which the reflection can be conducted' (2016: 297). Phenomenological questions are directed towards the 'lived meaning of a human phenomenon that is experientially recognizable and experientially accessible' (ibid.).

Despite the need to define the topics and aims of the research, in terms of the 'interviewer-traveller' idea, these should not be taken too narrowly. After all, it is essential to have an open attitude in the field of investigation and to walk a part of the way with the people there. For that, it is necessary to become aware of one's attitudes and preconceptions and put these aside or bracket them in the sense of epoché (Husserl [1936] 1970: 135–7). This bracketing as an attitude of suspension turns to the phenomenological given as it appears or shows itself. Researchers may have experiences in the field and conversations that astonish, irritate or even disappoint them. These experiences are learning experiences in the phenomenological sense, essential to generate insights and find their way into phenomenological texts (cf. Chapter 5).

Engaging with the dynamics of the respective research landscape opens up new questions and reveals relevant phenomena that are worth investigating. An experience log or research logbook helps record these aspects. It is also not uncommon for researchers to find their specific focus within the previously defined broader research topic only in the course of their experience in the research field. For instance, if the question is what pupils learn and experience over four years at a secondary school, it may be that working in the field leads to a narrower focus on the connection between learning and assessment. Thus, the Vignette and Anecdote Research Project at the University of Innsbruck generated studies on various facets of learning, such as attribution, finding or invention, curiosity or desire to know or grasping or being grasped.

In most cases, it will also be helpful to approach the phenomenon from a theoretical perspective and explore the state of knowledge on the topic in question. The next step is to develop an interview design. Which methods should be utilized? Are narrative interviews sufficient, or does a mixed-method approach make sense? Are interviews and discussions the most suitable way to generate answers to the questions posed? How many participants should be interviewed, how often and over what period of time?

A semi-structured questionnaire or non-structured interview aligns with the concept of the traveller. Regardless of the chosen type of interview, researchers will understand this as a guide rather than a catalogue of questions to work through. Focus group discussions are also well suited as a basis for anecdotes. However, anecdotes can also arise from more informal conversations and situations (see Section 4.2).

Brinkmann and Kvale (2018) point out that interview projects – perhaps research projects in general – are often characterized by 'a back-and-forth process'. Pilot interviews may show that the question guide needs to be adapted. Additionally, the theoretical discussion may lead to a new focus so that further interviews become necessary or previous interviews need to be revisited from different perspectives. In the case of anecdote research, it may be that the passages of conversation that enable the development of a scene or phenomenological text from them are rare and that further interviews are necessary.

4.2 Picking flowers by the wayside: The impromptu conversation

Anecdote research was initially developed and honed in a school context following the experience with vignette research. The gradual trialling and expansion of the method encouraged its application in other contexts, including various social spaces and different contexts. The first attempts generated vignettes about people waiting for the train at the station and anecdotes from conversations with young people in their free time. The dilation of the field was inspired, among other theoretical approaches, by the early research by Martha Muchow ([1935] 2012) on the lives of big city children, newly documented and published by Hannelore Faulstich-Wieland and Peter Faulstich (2012). The impromptu narratives by the Working Group Bielefelder Soziologen (1976) were a methodological starting point.

Improvised narratives can arise in structured research projects as well as in a free and open phenomenological research approach. They can result from a targeted research design, which does not consider structured interviews with audio recordings or even arise from spontaneous conversational situations. One example is a conversation with patients in a hospital where a focus group discussion had taken place with the medical staff about a patient-friendly health service organization. Upon leaving the meeting room, researchers are spontaneously engaged in conversation by two patients who are curious about what was happening in the room, which is visible through a glass wall. When the patients hear about the project, they spontaneously share their own experiences. The researchers ask whether they may include these stories in their research, and the two patients say yes and tell more stories. The situation would not be suitable for a structured interview; postponing and reconstructing the conversation in a structured setting would be at the expense of spontaneity. The exact transcript or recording of the conversation with the smartphone audio and notes on the bodily gestures extract valuable statements for an anecdote that can enrich the data material from the planned interviews with exciting insights.

Something similar happened in the course of the development of vignette research. After situations in the research field were perceived as meaningful for a vignette, sometimes structured interviews were conducted with the people concerned (Peterlini 2016c) and sometimes casual conversations about the situation that had just occurred or what had taken place the day before. The transcription of these conversations, including notes on body language, was deliberately not used to expand the context or decode the vignettes, as this could have led to an essentialist search for the truth behind the description. For example, if a child displayed behaviour in class that the researcher perceived as unsettling, it proved difficult if the child, when asked about it, dismissed the disconcerting situation as indifference or did not know what to say about the situation. The subsequent interviews, therefore, could not and should not be used to confirm, causally decipher or even falsify the contents of the vignette, as it reflected the researchers' shared experience. However, this data material proved to have value in its own right. An example from social space research in which the situation summarized in a vignette was initially experienced by a researcher:

> A man is sitting on a wide pavement leaning against the advertising pillar at the crossroads opposite the station building. He has placed two 1.5-litre Coke bottles, two smaller Thermos flasks and his rucksack in front of him. The policewoman standing by a patrol car in front of the station building looks briefly in the man's direction, turns round and speaks into the vehicle. Her colleague at the wheel gets out; they walk together across the zebra crossing to the advertising pillar and stand in front of the man crouching on the ground. They speak to the man – barely intelligible from a few metres away – he looks up and gesticulates, and now the policewoman points forward towards the city with an outstretched hand and says louder: 'There is a park there; you can sit there, not here.' The man gets up with some difficulty, stands opposite the policewoman, and spreads his arms – the policewoman and her companion point once more towards the city, then they turn away and walk back across the zebra crossing to the patrol car. The man looks after them briefly, follows them to the centre of the zebra crossing and shouts something after them. When the policewoman turns to him, he spreads his arms as if apologizing. She shrugs her shoulders and walks on. The man strolls back across the road, stands briefly in front of his rucksack, takes a few things out of his bulging jacket pockets, puts them next to the rucksack, then takes the first bottle of Coke and puts it in his pocket, then the second, then the two Thermos flasks. Finally, he shoulders the rucksack, takes a step in the direction he has been instructed, stops, looks back at the police, moves his hand up and down, grins and takes a few more steps. Then he speaks to a passer-by. 'Do you know what discrimination is?' The man smiles and shrugs his shoulders slightly. (Cennamo, Donlic and Peterlini 2020: 186–7)

This concludes the vignette. Immediately after the episode between the police and the man at the advertising column, there was a conversation with the researcher standing nearby, which resulted in an impromptu narrative. It is reproduced here partly verbatim and partly as a narrative description of the situation, as it could also be the basis for an anecdote.

Since I (the researcher) had come a little closer during the scene described in the vignette, I ask the man what he meant by discrimination. His answer:
'Doesn't that exist in Austria?'
I reply that there is discrimination everywhere and ask again what he means by that:
'They won't let me sit here, even though I haven't hurt anyone. It was a nice place here, with sunshine. I've been travelling through Europe for seven years, everywhere. It's nice in summer, but in winter … phew. Look at the shoes I'm wearing' (he's wearing lined rubber boots), 'in summer it's hot, and there is smell' (grabs his nose), 'but in the rain and in winter you need something like this, and I can't carry several pairs of shoes around, there has to be room for everything' He taps his rucksack with a grin. He continues: 'I experienced the worst winter, a bastard winter, shit, in Amsterdam, it was cold as hell. I've only been back to Germany once, but there …' (he grabs his neck, shakes himself …) 'No, that was not possible.'
Question: 'I thought you were from Germany?'
He smiles: 'That's why it didn't work … but why YOU, YOU, YOU?' He holds out his hand. 'I'm Klaus.' When I shake his hand and say my name and he hears 'Hans', he smiles, 'Hansi …' He is silent, then he says in a hushed tone:
'You have the same name as my father.'
'I see, and that is not good?'
'No, do you think if that were good, I would be here' he points down at his ragged trousers, a button has popped open on his fly, 'so … although my father, he just passes me by, the mother, that …' Silent, then without prompting, 'the mother was a whore', he looks at me firmly, the smile is frozen.
Question: 'As a profession? I mean, depending on national law, that is also a profession …'

He smiles and spreads his arms out again: 'She fucked, and then another child and another man came along. I have a father, if it is my father, because when I was seven, they told me you are not our child ...' he nods to himself '... yes and what are you doing ... at some point, your head will burst ...' he laughs, 'I have three, four stepfathers, the mother, you know the one, she weighed 150 kilos, she went to a party, she took me with her, then she fucked someone again and his wife found out, and then her son, my friend, told me, you, my mother is getting divorced, my father is now your stepfather. Yes, you have to go crazy at some point, it sucks, at some point you go crazy, yes, that's when I left, now I'm hiking, I've been hiking for seven years, at night I look for a place, in winter often an empty hut or something, and now I'm here, in Austria, I just wandered here, I want to stay here now, look for a job, I can do several jobs, I've grown weeds, in garden centres, I don't like doing that, but sometimes you just need money, I am a trained locksmith, I can also weld, I have done carpentry ... When I find work, I'll look for a flat, now my head is empty from hiking, yes I still smoke and drink, but I don't snort any more, you can count the lines I snort in a year on one hand, I do smoke a bit, drink too. Hey, when I was in Germany, I also saw my friends from before, they only snorted, snorted, yes, and when they aren't snorting anything, they sit in front of the computer ... Hey, we used to beat up fascists together, now they sit in front of the computer ... yes, what's that all about? We used to stand together; then we would see a fascist, and we'd all go after him and beat the pig ... Now ... sitting in front of the computer. That sucks' (He shows the pursuing and knocking on the head by taking a few quick steps and then hitting an imaginary fascist on the head with his clenched fist). 'Because you know, I have been an anarchist since I was 15', he rolls up his sleeve and shows the symbol tattooed on his right forearm. Then he takes the rucksack, holds his hand to me, 'What is your name again, oh yes, Hansi', and leaves. (Author 2020, unpublished)

The vignette that preceded this conversation tells nothing about the man's subjective narrative, nor can it be supplemented or corrected by it. It speaks for itself, not about the man's story but about how regulations of social space permit certain uses (the parking of cars in front of the station) and prohibit others (sitting down in front of an advertising pillar); they hierarchize power relations and allocate the right to expel. Likewise, the vignette offers possibilities of interpretation in the field of tension between order and resistance, which is shown – partly across the street – in the gestures, attitudes and movements that occur between the police and the man in front of the advertising pillar, for example in his attempt to defend his position and ultimately to give way, but not without a residual attitude of resistance. (Cennamo, Donlic and Peterlini 2020: 188)

While the vignette thus allows considerations, reflections and statements about power relations and structures in the public sphere without the subjective biographical background, impromptu narratives reveal other levels of interpretation. In an open understanding of hermeneutics, no absolute and final understanding is expected but rather a 'different understanding' (Danner 2006: 71; Danner 1995). The man's story, thus, should not objectivize the depiction in the vignette or point to an objective truth but rather enable further understandings, other irritations and assertions on other (pedagogical) questions. When processed into an anecdote, they can stimulate insights and reflection for biographical research:

Anecdote 7

Klaus complains that he was sent away by the police from the square in front of the advertising pillar at the station. He gathers his things together: 'They won't let me sit here, even though I have not done anything to anyone. It was a nice place here, with sunshine. I've been travelling through Europe for seven years, everywhere. It's nice in summer, but in winter ... phew. Look at the shoes I'm wearing' (he is wearing lined rubber boots), 'in summer it's hot, and there's smell' (grabs his nose), 'but in the rain and in winter you need something like this, and I can't carry several pairs of shoes around, there has to be room for everything' – he taps his rucksack with a grin. He continues: 'I experienced the worst winter, a bastard winter, shit, in Amsterdam, it was cold as hell. I've only been back to Germany once, but there ...' (he grabs his neck, shakes himself ...) 'No, that wasn't possible.' When asked why he could not stay in Germany, he recounts his encounter with friends from the past: 'Hey, we used to beat up fascists together, now they're sitting in front of the computer ... yeah, what's that all about? We used to stand together; then we would see a fascist, and we'd all go after him and beat the pig ... Now ... sitting in front of the computer. That sucks.' He takes a few quick steps, extends his hand, clenches his fist and punches it up and down several times. Then he laughs out loud. 'Because you know, I have been an anarchist since I was 15', he rolls up his sleeve and shows the symbol tattooed on his right forearm. Then he takes the rucksack, holds out his hand to me and leaves. (Author, 7 August 2019, unpublished)

4.3 The importance of body and response

Why do we prefer the term conversation over interview in anecdote research? The conversational situation between researchers and research partners bears many similarities to that of a (qualitative) interview. An interview, a conversation or a spontaneous interaction between two individuals is a communicative setting where the relationship between the conversational partners is clearly defined and not interchangeable; one person, the researcher, asks questions, and the other person, the participant or research partner, responds to them. The scope of responses varies and is primarily determined by the nature of the questions. Nevertheless, anecdote researchers prefer to use the term 'conversation'. This term emphasizes the openness of the situation and the effort of the researchers to engage in a dialogue with the research partners that deserves the name, meaning to interact with them on an equal footing, where the respondents not only answer posed questions but also respond to demands in a question–answer process, and vice versa, where questioning can also be interpreted as responding to demands. 'Responding is not something else, namely, a response to an external demand, but giving a response is more than simply passing on existing knowledge from the beginning, precisely because a response can be refused' (Waldenfels 2007a: 192).

Of course, this aspect can never be completely ignored in an interview situation, but it is more or less limited by the more fixed allocation of roles, the interview guide and the question. In conversations, on the other hand, varied and unexpected responses from both sides are desired. It is considered a quality of the conversation if it does not take the expected course or that dictated by the question guide. Instead, it may occur, for example, that the experts – albeit initially inspired by a question or a conversation impulse – start talking of their own accord and thereby influence the course of the conversation or if the researchers deviate from the planned questions. The entire responsibility of the participants in their verbal, acoustic, emotional and, above all, bodily articulations is affected in the question–answer process. The concept of *conversation* considers that experience is not only expressed in *what* is told but, above all, in *how* it is told. This idea about conversation as an event of question and answer also influences the understanding and writing of anecdotes, in which not only verbal aspects are reproduced or formulated but non-verbal, primarily bodily aspects of the conversation are also included (see Chapter 5).

Waldenfels speaks of the in-between between question and answer, which arises in the dialogue between claim and answer. This in-between is no longer attributable to either of the two dialogue partners. The result is a network of the familiar and the strange. The connecting and the dividing moments create space for a surplus and a claim that comes from elsewhere and disrupts the situation (see Waldenfels 2000: 299). This idea reveals the potential of a conversation in which information is not simply retrieved but in which the participants are engaged and challenged by the presence, behaviour and statements of the other person and contribute to the conversation in a responsive, creative-constructive way. Such an attitude can lead to a situation in which researchers and experts are surprised by their statements, emotions and bodily articulations, in which their claims or those of the other person trigger irritation, resistance, astonishment or perplexity, in which they invite a flood of words or silence. All of this is valued as an essential component and expression of the lived experience in the understanding of the dialogue between researchers and experts and is later included by the researchers as a data source for recording the incomprehensible, namely the lived and remembered experiences in the investigations.

This makes it clear that anecdote researchers are not interested in merely recounting or retelling the remembered and recounted experiences but in reproducing them in as unaltered a form as possible. Just as it is not possible – as already discussed – for people to have direct access to their experiences in the past and simply recall them, it is likewise impossible to exclude the dialogue situation, the question–answer dynamic between researchers and interviewees and to depict the remembered and recounted experiences in a *purified* form. However, this circumstance, the manifold *refraction* and alteration of previous experiences, is not only seen as a loss: in anecdotes, the remembered and narrated experience of the experts, as well as the experience of the conversation, can come alive in a condensed form and take on new expressive shape. Just as memory contains elements of recalling and new creation, the question–answer process is also permeated by the past and the present, by answers that have both repetitive and new creative elements. *What* is remembered and *how* it is remembered is fundamentally determined by the present, in this case, also by the conversation's situation and by the researcher's questions and impulses. In this respect, remembering is to be understood as an answer to a claim, as a response to a question, to the other person and the situation of the conversation, and as an answer to the claim of the past self and its experience.

Van Manen draws attention to the particular challenge of interviews in phenomenological studies: 'It is much easier to get a person to tell *about* an experience than to tell an experience as lived through' (2016: 315). Interviewees often give opinions and assessments of experiences. To increase the chance of hearing about lived experiences, some aspects need to be taken into account (ibid.):

1. As described in Section 4.2, more informal situations and places are often better suited to narrating experiences. Van Manen recommends, for example, 'the kitchen table' or 'a coffee shop' as suitable places.
2. A trusting relationship is crucial for determining whether dialogue partners talk about lived experiences. It is, therefore, important not to 'open the door' straight away but to take time to get in touch with each other, build trust and then move on to the topic or phenomenon to be investigated. A co-experiential attitude in the conversation is characterized by researchers showing interest, listening, giving time to answer, enduring silence, asking questions

without probing and approaching their conversation partner with their heart and soul.
3. Certain questions are better or less suited for inviting dialogue partners to talk about lived experiences and gain rich and concrete answers or stories. Open questions are suitable at first: *What comes to mind? What events or situations do you remember in particular? Can you give me an example?* For specific events or situations, it may be essential to ask: *What was it like for you? What exactly happened? What did you or others say or do? How did it make you feel? What did you think? What do you still remember?* (See van Manen 2016: 316). Ultimately, it is about getting as close as possible to the experience and less about hearing explanations or interpretations. At the same time, perspectives on experiences, what is remembered and forgotten and the evaluation of experiences should be seen as part of this process and, therefore, also as valuable results or data.
4. Van Manen recommends not being afraid of silence. For example, repeating the last question or the interviewer's answer in a questioning tone of voice can help with possible blockages (ibid.: 316).

4.4 First steps from the transcription to an anecdote

In anecdote research, the interviews and conversations are also recorded on a sound recorder, as is usual for an empirical approach. An exception to this can be impromptu conversations, which cannot always be recorded but are sometimes written down by hand as verbatim as possible during or immediately after the conversation (see Section 4.3). Consent to the recording by the interviewees is just as much a scientific standard as careful handling of the tapes and transcriptions regarding data protection is; names are anonymized or converted into nicknames during transcription. The same may be necessary for any information identifying the narrator or the persons named by him or her. The transcription is carried out as closely as possible to the text; pause lengths, special emphases and linguistic anomalies are taken into account by standard transcription rules. One open question is how to deal with conversations conducted in dialect. Maintaining the dialect complicates the transcription, as there is usually no standardized spelling for dialectal pronunciations and word formations. Consequently, the transcription could be more arbitrary and complex for outsiders to read later. As with other methodological approaches to interviews conducted in dialect, it is possible to convert dialectal speech into the respective standard language. However, phrases or emphases in dialect with particular emotional content should be preserved. It is equally important to record paralinguistic moments and to supplement the transcription with perceptions of bodily expressions, such as posture, gestures, tempo of movements, facial expressions, position of the hands, position and change of position of the legs.

The transcribed interview, enriched by the observations during the conversation, can now be used to develop anecdotes. For this purpose, the transcripts and interview notes are read several times with a mindset open to being affected and responding; a sequenced approach is unnecessary. Instead, engaging with what happens between the researcher and the text is essential. This means, on the one hand, not only being guided by what particularly draws the eye but also paying attention to passages that were skipped or skimmed through to look at them again. In cases of doubt, the audio recording can always be consulted, for instance, if there is uncertainty as to whether the voice became shrill from agitation or hoarseness during a particular statement. It can also be helpful to look at the notes taken during the conversation or visualize the situation again to see how a violent outstretching of the hand relates to the text and the situation at the time. Was it anger or passion? Or something completely different? Or was it just a fly being swatted away (which can still be meaningful if it happens at a particular point in the conversation, while the fly was previously allowed to crawl around unnoticed on the arm)?

In this way, the transcript and the notes become more and more comprehensible, and the linguistic and metalinguistic content takes on new structures beyond the chronological sequence: where do spoken words and physical utterances develop a particularly meaningful expressiveness? Where do they seem to contradict each other? Do the outlines of a story which can be condensed into an anecdote emerge from the conversation's transcript?

In this process, researchers need to allow themselves to be surprised: a researcher can be interested in the phenomenon of power, for example, and tend to look for it when the interviewee talks about the behaviour of her superiors or parents. Then, however, she mentions an initially inconspicuous passage from the text in which the person clenches her fist and talks about an idea that has recently occurred to her and which she is determined to pursue. The result could be an anecdote on empowerment, such as overcoming powerlessness in the face of a restrictive situation, which had been expressed at other points in the interview. However, other phenomena, such as frustration or joy, may also emerge. They are part of the phenomenological surplus and can be treasures that enrich one's academic work as phenomena of power, powerlessness and empowerment.

Such text passages can be marked on the transcription manuscript with coloured pencils, circling them with a pen or bolding or colouring them on the digital manuscript. The following example, which Silvia Krenn (2020) has prepared for a methodological guide, is a seven-minute excerpt from a research discussion lasting around half an hour between the researcher (Q) and the pupil Brigitta (S2). It is an extract from which an anecdote was generated; parts of the text used verbatim in the anecdote are highlighted. The interview was designed for research on school learning experiences and focused on the past school years and the individual school subjects. The first question refers to the researcher's observation of Brigitta during her fieldwork.

Transcript excerpt (Krenn 2020: 100–2).

Q   You wrote that together very quickly #mhm# or finished it then, the exercise. And I still remember what you said: you're a fast A student. ((S2 laughs)) Many years ago, four years ago. Is that still the case? Or #yes, I was top of the class last year# how has that developed? Sorry?

S2 I was top of the school last year with two other girls. Yes, because we all got straight As in our school reports.

Q   Oh (.), great! #yes# (.) and when you think back to these last few years, what have you learnt that you can do differently now, better, let's think about the subjects we've seen, German, maths.

S2 Yes, maths, I've really improved. **So I've got much better there, and it's easier for me now,** and I, but maths is also **my favourite** subject, so that's how it is. ((smiles)) And in (.) English last year, we had a project speech, there was someone from Africa, and he was with us for a week and we did it with him, and I also spoke freely in English, because he didn't know any German, so a bit, but we spoke English with him. And he understood me too, and I was able to speak freely, so I had the confidence to do so, and then he saw that I could do it and all and so on. And that's actually nice. And with the essays in German, for example, I also learnt something and so on.

Q mh, what exactly did you learn there, with the essays, for example?

S2 Yes, the formulations, expressions, because I've had a few mistakes in expression and so on and then I've learnt that now, and now I've had a few, three comma mistakes in the last school assignment. ((laughs)) But now I've practised it again at home and then I think I can do it now anyway.

Q mh, yes, and you said that maths is much better. What exactly is much better there, too?

S2 yes, the quicker understanding and then learning and when I study for tests, I write it all very quickly, very quickly, and then I can do it. and I can also write 2 or 3 pages in an hour, and that's much easier for me. when she explains something new, so when Mrs Saxinger explains something new,

Q mh, then it's easier for you to understand and remember that, isn't it?

S2 yes, exactly

Q Writing, you also said, #yes# goes so quickly, mh (.) And how did you learn that? You said, yes, that's what I learnt. And how exactly did you learn that?

S2 in maths, we have, well, there is the frontal instruction and that, but we don't have frontal instruction. We do everything: we sit down together somewhere in the back in the seating area, and she explains it to us, or we go to a learning island or outside, and she explains it to us on the floor or outside the school if the weather is nice. And this is also much better for me somehow, because then you learn it faster and understand it better, because then she also shows it here and with some, she takes some example, she always has some ropes with her or something to show us. And so on.

Q That's in maths now, isn't it? #Yes# Mh. So the small groups, #mh# and the individual showing and the visualization
S2 and we also have weekly plans, so we have to organize everything ourselves. And that's really good for me personally, I always finish quickly. I also do things at home. Others (.) take a bit longer, or they're lazier, but they still manage. And yes.
Q mh. So in maths, there are, the lessons are simply better for your learning, and what do you learn at home or how do you study at home?
S2 Yes, as I said, we have weekly plans, and I always read through everything again, and then I do a few more examples, and then I also look to see which ones are not on the weekly plan, and then I sometimes do them and so on. That's also in German. In German we sometimes have weekly plans and sometimes homework and so on, and that actually works very well.
S2 In maths, I'm interested in maths anyway and I also like to do maths, **if I see something somewhere, I quickly work it out and so on. It's just like that.** And (..) Yes (…)
Q Yes, and when you were in maths, was it always like that in maths? That, that, that you had such enthusiasm, #so# I realize now that you're really #yes! ((enthusiastic)) #are enthusiastic, #yes, so# that you don't just learn it at school, but that you also apply it #yes# and that you carry it around with you.
S2 Yes, **I've always liked maths, but now it's somehow better because it's easier for me to understand** and I enjoy it more because, for example, with Sandra (laughs) – she's always like that with me, we're like, how do you say it (.), like in a competition, so the two of us against each other, who finishes faster and so on. And yes, she sometimes explains things to me, I explain things to her, so I often talk to her on the phone and do maths at the same time. She does maths, I do maths, and then ((laughs)) on my mobile phone.
Q So you said she's your friend #best friend#, best friend and with her it's also fun again # mh, with her all subjects are actually fun, she's always doing something, she often laughs a lot. ((laughs)) (.) and you like that. mh. ok, but there hasn't been any incident where you say, yes, that was actually in maths, because Sandra hasn't been there that long, has she?
S2 mh, she's been there since the second grade.

Q she's been there since the second grade, so two and a half years soon.mh. Yes, but maths is your favourite subject, you said.
S2 mh. yes, the best thing for me in maths was how we did it, **prime factorization, because I was the fastest there (smiles)** We had a competition on the blackboard. **I already had so much ((laughs)). was finished, the other one still had so little. ((laughs)) I thought it was funny because we often do competitions like that or relay races in groups and so on. So maths with lots of fun and movement.** We also always have a race around the school on the weekly schedule, so we do a bit of exercise. (T4BS2)

These highlights are the result of a longer process. The phenomenological search movements in the interview are orientated towards places where lived experiences emerge from memory or narration. In this case, the following anecdote emerged from this section of the interview:

Anecdote 8

Maths is Brigitta's favourite subject. 'Well, it is!' she states emphatically and smiles challengingly. She has always liked maths, and she also likes to calculate. 'If I see something somewhere, I quickly work it out', she says passionately. She almost stumbles at the words, beaming all over her face. 'It's just the way it is'. In the four years at the new secondary school, she has really improved in maths. 'I've got much better at maths, and it's easier for me now', she says proudly. Moreover, she talks excitedly about the prime factorization competition. 'I was the fastest', Brigitta laughs mischievously. The teacher explained the material, and Brigitta quickly understood it. Then, there was a competition on the blackboard in pairs – always one against the other. 'I have already had so many', she bursts out laughing before continuing, 'I was finished; the other one still had so few! She almost rolls her eyes at the idea: 'I thought it was funny'. And again, serious and in control: 'We often do competitions like this or relay races in groups – maths with lots of fun and movement. (4BS2-A5, Krenn 2020: 97–8)

How to organize the writing process from transcript to anecdote and what to take into account are explained in more detail and theoretically substantiated in the following chapter.

CHAPTER 5

From transcript to anecdote

This chapter introduces anecdote writing and explains how to edit transcribed interviews and conversations. How can meaningful connections be made between different passages? How are personal perceptions regarding bodily interactivity during the interview brought into the anecdote? How should the anecdote's theme, focus and punchline be brought out? At this step, we speak of a raw anecdote, which has to undergo an intersubjective validation process in research groups to test and hone it.

The process of writing down the experiences remembered and recounted in the conversations with the researchers in the form of anecdotes deserves special attention. In their essay 'An Event of Sound', Carina Henrikkson and Tone Saevi (2009) highlight the strengths of the written representation of lived experiences in literary texts. They point out that in these texts, be they anecdotes or other experimental (written) forms of representation, the lived experience remains alive or comes (back) to life in a particular way that also allows readers direct access to these experiences (see ibid.: 35). The metaphor *an event of sound* points in particular to the sonic qualities of texts, which are suitable for expressing qualities of lived experience, which is always already past experience and which we are always too late to capture, qualities that may easily go lost in conventional forms of academic writing. According to the authors, researchers move in the borderland between a poetic attitude and a writing style orientated towards the pragmatic (cf. ibid.). Henriksson and Saevi compare this type of writing with the work of artists, who succeed in illuminating the essence of things in their artwork (see ibid.: 37).

An anecdote speaks to us much in the same way as a good novel or a beautiful poem does. It evokes feelings of recognition, points to experiential possibilities that we have never encountered before, or leads to thoughts whose possibility we were not earlier aware of.
... the intention of a phenomenologist is to have the reader receive and respond to the otherwise concealed meaning of the lived experience which can be evoked in the honed anecdote. (Ibid.: 38)

It is about making a meaning tangible 'which we are unable to express clearly in any other way' (Kockelmans 1987: ix; as cited in Henriksson and Saevi 2009: 38). With reference to Martin Heidegger (2005), Henriksson and Saevi emphasize that the only way for people to really say something is 'to listen and respond to the things of the world through language, to let language itself speak' (Henriksson and Saevi 2009: 38). 'The vocation, or call, of a text, is sensed as an implicit, felt understanding that is non-cognitive as well as cognitive, sensed as well as reflected' (ibid.: 38–9).

In this way, phenomenological texts represent a connection between the lived experiences they evoke and the reader's experiences. As an *event of sound*, they appeal to readers, their hearing, their thinking and their bodies and make it possible for lived experiences, also in their physical dimension, to be brought back to life while reading.

According to Henriksson and Saevi, writing phenomenological texts is like an adventure with an open outcome. Intentionality and a planned approach seem to do more harm than good to this endeavour: 'To enter the world of lived experiences through the world of language is to embark on an adventurous endeavour, which sometimes proves to be an amazing discovery as the meaning of an experience unfolds before our eyes, on paper or the screen. However, there is an ironic paradox in writing for discovery: we discover nothing at all' (ibid.: 52). In *Writing in the Dark* (2002), van Manen points out the difficulties researchers can encounter when translating experiences into language. It is not uncommon that 'every word kills and becomes the death of the object it tries to represent' (ibid.: 244). Capturing and representing lived experiences in the form of phenomenological texts enters uncertain terrain and is threatened by constant failure. This phenomenon is not least due to the ambivalent, even paradoxical, relationship between lived experience and its expression. Modesty is therefore appropriate for the claim to help experience find expression, as Henriksson and Saevi also point out in their concluding plea:

> To ask of phenomenology that it makes anything or everything clear is to remain in the realm of Husserl's transcendental phenomenology, where essence precedes existence. But there is no original meaning, just possible meanings and shadows on the wall of the cave, which we as researchers can try to describe, interpret, and bestow meaning upon. Hermeneutic phenomenology is not a romantic project; it is very much a realistic project. It is an exploration into the lifeworld – the puzzling, the complex, and sometimes the unintelligible world we live in and experiences we live through. The phenomenon is not a meaning but a thing, a substance. (Henriksson and Saevi 2009: 53)

However, the difficulty of expressing what we want to say, and the fact that language always lags behind experience or threatens to distort and falsify it, should not discourage researchers; on the contrary, 'it urges us, forces us, and pushes us to write evocatively of lived experiences – with even more careful circumspection – and deeper devotion' (Henriksson and Saevi 2009: 54).

5.1 Selecting relevant conversational turns from co-experience

There are different approaches to phenomenological research with anecdotes. In the concept of van Manen (1990: 68–70), researchers write anecdotes based on 'close observation', which in vignette and anecdote research would lead to rather detailed descriptions for vignette writing. Another approach of van Manen consists of anecdotes written by people in the first person about their own experiences (ibid.).

In the method of anecdote research, as presented in this volume, anecdotes are written by the researchers. Both approaches provide valuable access to remembered experiences. Why can it be useful for researchers to write anecdotes based on interviews or conversations? Not all people whose experiences are engaging for research can express themselves in writing in a nuanced way and put remembered experiences on paper as a 'good story'. Van Manen also points out that many prefer to talk about their experiences orally (see 1990: 68). In particular, anecdotes about focus group discussions would be a complex challenge for the participants and can be better written by researchers.

Using the example of an anecdote that captures the remembered experiences of thirteen–fourteen-year-old pupils at the end of their secondary school years, the process from transcript to anecdote will be demonstrated:

Anecdote 9

When the pupils think back to their four years at secondary school, the name of a teacher who taught them English in Year 1 and Year 2 comes up again and again. 'And we didn't have so much fun with her. We didn't get much into our heads', explains Kerim. 'She gave us an assignment, took her book, sat down, and we sat up for hours to ask questions; she didn't explain anything to us.' He gets upset. 'And then she said: "I'll explain it to you tomorrow"', Konuk interjects. Mrs Keller has been teaching English in the class since year three. Everything is very different with her. 'When we do something, she shares the task, she explains it two or three times, she immediately realizes when we're not getting anywhere', raves Kerim. During the lesson, the teacher goes around the class and checks whether the tasks are completed. If there are any difficulties, she helps the pupils. 'She works with us', beams Karl. (Ammann et al. 2017: 195)

When writing anecdotes, researchers endeavour not only to write down *what* is said but, above all, to describe *how* something is said: Does a dialogue partner stammer, does the flow of speech falter, does the gaze become fixed or is it directed towards the floor, does the breath quicken? Body expression often tells us more and sometimes something different than the proverbial *1000 words*. In the example above, the verbs that describe the quality of the statements, such as tone of voice, emotions or facial expressions, are particularly striking: Kerim *gets upset* when he talks about a previous teacher, he *raves* about the English teacher who now teaches them, Karl *beams* when he talks about working together. Experience comes to life in storytelling, and experience urges expression thanks to the co-experience attitude during the conversation (Chapter 4). Only the researcher who conducted the conversation can decide on the selection and suitability of the words used. It is helpful to (re) listen to the transcript to remember non-verbal and metalinguistic elements and the atmosphere of the conversation.

The text passages from the conversations used as the basis for writing an anecdote are selected according to what affected the researchers in the conversation, what came to the fore and what stood out or attracted attention from what was said. An anecdote often begins with the question that prompted the story or statement to make the context or topic clear to the reader.

Here is an extract from the transcript of the focus group discussion that formed the basis for the above anecdote:

Q:	… English did you want? #00:01:38–5#
Kerim:	Yes. #00:01:39-7#
Q:	O.k. Why English? #00:01:42-7#
Kerim:	Because a lot has changed. #00:01:44-3#
Q:	What has changed? #00:01:46-5#
Kerim:	Yes, we used to have a different teacher. #00:01:46-5#
Q:	Ahh, until the second grade or so? #00:01:49-4#
Kerim:	Yes, we had a teacher in first and second grade, her name was Ms Krumm. And we didn't have so much fun with her …, we didn't get much into our heads. #00:01:59-5#
Q:	Yes. #00:02:00-8#
Kerim:	And now #00:02:01-1#
Q:	Didn't learn much? #00:01:58-4#
Kerim, 2, 3:	No ((several at the same time)) #00:02:03-3#
Kerim:	For example, I could give you an example, she gave us a task, took her book, sat down and we sat down for hours to ask questions, she didn't explain anything to us, she just #submitted# #00:02:15-1#
Konuk:	#and then she (?), then she said, but it was short #00:02:17-3#
Kerim:	Just take the sheet of paper #00:02:18-8#
Konuk:	then (?) she said, I'll explain tomorrow. #00:02:20-8#

Kerim:	She just presented the sheet and then, she just read the book that she had. #00:02:24-2#
Q:	O.K. #00:02:25-7#
Kerim:	And it's much different with Ms Keller. For example, when we do something, she shares the task, she explains it two or three times, she immediately realizes if we're not getting anywhere, she asks us herself #00:02:40-6#
Q:	mhm. #00:02:40-6#
Kerim:	She goes through every time, through the class and sees if we're doing it or not and always helps. #00:02:43-4#
Q:	o.k. #00:02:43-4#
Kerim:	Yes. #00:02:46-6#
Karl:	She works with us. #00:02:47-6#
Q:	So you're learning more now? #00:02:48-3#
Kerim, 2, 3:	Yes. #00:02:50-7#
Konuk:	Much more. #00:02:50-8#
Kerim:	#It's also more fun #00:02:50-8# #00:02:50-8#
Konuk:	#I've even improved my grade. #00:02:53-8#

The circumstances of the conversation (space and time), the inner and outer attitude and the relationship of the dialogue partners, the questions asked and many other influences will determine *what* and *how* events are remembered and spoken out. When writing the anecdotes, the aim is to preserve these aspects as far as possible and to use the (shared) experience of the conversation as an additional source of knowledge.

The pupils talk about the changes brought about by a change of teacher in English. What is remarkable about this interview excerpt is that the group of students determines the topic; it is obviously important to them to tell the researcher about their experiences. The narrative flow is hardly interrupted by the researcher, for example, by (follow-up) questions. The fact that the students tell this story right at the beginning of the interview reinforces the impression of the importance of the experience for the group. The significance of statements can be sensed particularly in a co-experiential attitude. The intensity with which the pupils narrate the story may have affected the researcher and driven them to select this sequence for an anecdote. Another reason for the selection is usually research interest. The research project in which this interview took place addressed mainly the following questions: What are the students' learning experiences? What do they experience during their time at secondary school? What do they remember, and how? How do they respond to expectations?

How this transcript and the students' statements became an anecdote is explained later.

5.2 Highlighting one experience, one theme and one focus

Anecdotes are generally characterized, among other things, by their conciseness; they are short, simple stories that depict an event and contain a climax or punchline. Phenomenological anecdotes also exhibit this characteristic of the literary genre as a research tool. The requirement to include only one experience and one topic in an anecdote helps select suitable narrative sequences and encourages researchers to refrain from digressing and to keep the text concise.

Only rarely do interviewees tell ready-made stories or anecdotes that the researcher would only need to transcribe one-to-one. The young people in our example do not do this either. They add to the statements of others, interrupting each other. The task of the researcher is now to put these pieces together into a story or an anecdote in such a way that what moves and touches the pupils here, the lived and remembered experience, is expressed in such a way that this experience and the situation of the conversation become understandable to the reader. By creating the anecdote from different passages of the transcription, researchers avoid combining passages that are too separated in time into one text. The researcher should preserve the temporal unity and the narrative course of the conversation as far as possible; summarizing statements from different phases and contents of the conversation would be too much of an intrusion into the remembered experience of the conversation partners. Exceptions are conceivable if a topic or experience is brought up again later in the interview.

The entire transcript of the focus group discussion, from which the sequence above is taken, is thirty-three pages long – the interview lasted thirty-six minutes. The interview section used for the anecdote appears self-contained; the remainder deals with other topics. The experience that the students talk about in the anecdote is, on the one hand, that they felt left to fend for themselves in class with the previous English teacher and therefore understood and learned little; on the other hand, they now experience English lessons with a new teacher as positive and conducive to learning. The theme of the anecdote could be 'Good and bad experiences with teachers' or 'How the behaviour of teachers affects pupils' enjoyment of learning'.

5.3 Structuring a cogent and concise story

What makes a good story? What rules are helpful for writing an anecdote? The instructions for writing good stories are similar to cooking recipes; both can be helpful, but the ingredients for a captivating story can be grasped in fragments, just like the ingredients of a dish that delights our palate.

Van Manen describes the narrative style characteristics of an anecdote in a pointed way:

1. An anecdote is a very short and simple story.
2. An anecdote usually describes a single incident.
3. An anecdote begins close to the central moment of the experience.
4. An anecdote includes important concrete details.
5. An anecdote often contains several quotes (what was said, done and so on).
6. An anecdote closes quickly after the climax or when the incident has passed.
7. An anecdote often has an effective or 'punchy' last line: it creates punctum. (van Manen 2016: 251)

These characteristics can also serve as a guideline for writing phenomenological anecdotes. At the same time, adhering to them does not guarantee that an anecdote will succeed in expressing remembered experiences.

With reference to Roland Barthes (1981), Henriksson and Saevi (2009: 39) emphasize the necessary characteristic of a punch line (*punctum*) for a phenomenological text, 'to point out the particular meaning of something and establish a punctum'. According to Barthes, the characteristic of the *punctum* constitutes the difference between a snapshot and a photograph. No photographic image can represent the original, but the photograph, unlike the snapshot, is able to 'prick us, touch us, disturb us, move us, and address us' (ibid.: 40). The authors, referring to van Manen, attribute similar potential to the anecdote, which draws us into the event and at the same time forces us to reflect, which tells us something about 'a particular experience, a unique person, or an individual life' (ibid.: 39) and at the same time reveals 'something universal' (ibid.). The art of writing a coherent and experiential anecdote lies in the balance between faithfulness to the narrated experiences of research partners and the endeavour to express these experiences concisely and stirringly.

Another anecdote from the research project at secondary schools illustrates this endeavour:

Anecdote 10

Yes, in first grade, I was kind of an outsider because I studied a lot and all that. And the others didn't. They fought their way through with threes and fours. Back then, Klaus founded a fan club for Kevin and managed to get Kevin to become class president. He also kept a folder in which he documented all kinds of incidents at school. I did all sorts of rubbish in the first class. ... And now I do not do that any more, yes, studying, that hasn't changed, but because of the HTL[1] and so on, er, now they have actually accepted me. (Ammann et al. 2017: 189)

Let us take a closer look at the structure of the anecdote. The text begins without an introduction, with a statement from the pupil who describes his role as an outsider in the class at the time. Klaus explains that he had 'studied a lot', while 'the others' found school success less important. These statements in direct speech lead the reader directly into the narrative. We can only guess the question that provided the impetus (*what has changed in you and your study habits since first grade?*); moreover, we do not know if such a question was asked at all because an explicit question is foregone in favour of a more direct introduction. In the following few sentences, the narrator talks about Klaus's various first-grade activities. The idea of a ten-year-old founding a fan club for a classmate and using it to lobby or record school events is astonishing.

The anecdote also provides the following points to help determine whether to use direct or narrative speech: which of the interlocutor's statements are particularly emphasized? Are they accompanied by body language expressions that indicate their meaning? Which parts of the conversation are particularly rich in content and concise and would lose their expressiveness if converted into indirect speech? The anecdote concludes with a direct quote from Klaus, in which he, as a thirteen-year-old looking back, describes his involvement as 'rubbish'. This assessment could be provoking; it appears as a – perhaps surprising – twist or punchline. The effect is reinforced by the fact that Klaus talks about how he still studies (a lot) but otherwise behaves rather inconspicuously.

Last but not least, he attributes the fact that the others have now accepted him to his decision to attend a technical college. This closes the circle, with the initial situation ('in first grade I was kind of an outsider') changing over time at school ('now they have actually accepted me'). How this change process can be assessed, for instance, whether normalization processes are at work here, could be worked out in a *reading* (this will be discussed in Chapter 6).

5.4 Intersubjective validation of raw anecdotes

The first version of an anecdote, the *raw anecdote*, is ideally validated and enriched in dialogue with a research group and in intersubjective writing processes. Researchers without a research group should at least discuss and validate the texts in detail with another person. Except for impromptu narratives, the transcripts and audio recordings of the conversations or interviews serve for validation. The following questions help with validation:

1. Does the narrative remain close to what is said and narrated?
2. How is the physical (facial expressions, gestures, posture, breathing, tone of voice, pauses and so on) expressed? In

what posture, with what facial expressions, tone of voice and at what speed was something said? Was there a sigh, faster breathing, a particular emphasis? How can this be expressed linguistically?
3. Are the elements 'one theme, one experience, one focus, one punchline' considered?
4. Is the text understandable, or should contextual information be included and processes described in more detail?
5. Do the quotes contain central statements? What can be described in narrative speech, and what should be reproduced in direct speech?
6. Which verbs of saying and meaning are used? Which verbs could convey the tone and expression of what is being said more accurately?
7. Have you succeeded in structuring a compelling and concise story? How can the arc of suspense and punchline be worked out even better while at the same time maintaining the closeness to the narrated and remembered experience?

It can be beneficial if colleagues in the research group rewrite or paraphrase the anecdote based on the audio file and the transcript. The different versions are read aloud, and the author then decides whether to replace their text with one of the versions or use ideas and text passages for their version.

For comparison, here is the first version of the anecdote about Klaus's stories:

> In first grade, Klaus didn't have such a good standing in the class. 'Yes, in first grade, I was kind of an outsider because I studied a lot and all that. And the others didn't. They fought their way through with Cs and Ds' (line 705–9). The thing with the Kevin fan club (Klaus founded a fan club for Kevin and managed to get him to become class president) and the folder in which Klaus documented all kinds of incidents at school also led to him being seen as an outsider. 'And now I do not do that any more, yes, studying, that hasn't changed, but because of the HTL and so on,

er, now they have actually accepted me' (line 722 f.). But Klaus still does not have a real friend in the class.

Some ideas that emerged during a recursive writing process in the research group were incorporated. For example, the first sentence was deleted, the somewhat cumbersome wording in the middle section was shortened, and the last sentence was omitted. The validation process makes clear that a conclusion would grant the context about Klaus's real friendships more importance than his narration and self-image.

It is usually a longer process until the anecdote is finished, and the revised texts are discussed again in the group, resulting in several versions. It is also advisable to keep older versions in order to reuse any original formulations or to be able to trace the validation and writing process.

Note

1 HTL stands for *Höhere technische Lehr- und Versuchsanstalt*, a higher vocational school following compulsory schooling (upper secondary level).

CHAPTER 6

Resonance reading and reflecting upon anecdotes

The method of analysing anecdotes, parallel to vignette research, is called *resonance reading*. What at first glance sounds simple, possibly even banal, is a multi-layered, complex process of understanding, finding meaning and reflection that can be organized in many different ways. After being extracted from conversations and woven into the text, the anecdotes are read in different settings and often from different perspectives. Once again, the phenomenological research approach is essential. The aim is not to reconstructively determine the approximate truth of the experiences summarized in the anecdote or to make definitive statements about them.

Similarly, the readings aim not to uncover a hidden meaning or refute a manifest significance. Instead, by reading the anecdote and analysing its content, the researchers attempt to uncover its multifaceted potential for meaning. Reading an anecdote is neither a linear nor a precisely sequenced process. The readers relate to the content of the anecdotes, allow themselves to be affected by individual passages or even just words and try to comprehend how they gain meaning by engaging with them. The emerging interpretations are not set absolutely but are picked up as a possibility of understanding, suggested and reflected upon in terms of its potential goals of insight.

The following sections set out the theoretical foundations of reading as a method of interpretation and explain the methodological steps to make anecdotes fruitful as instruments for generating knowledge through reflection.

6.1 Reading anecdotes from theoretical perspectives

The traditional requirement for empirical data analysis is a systematized and sequenced approach. In the foundation of the phenomenological method, Husserl explicitly turns away from this: 'Our investigation can, however, only proceed securely, if it repeatedly breaks with such systematic sequence … We search, as it were, in zigzag fashion' (Husserl [1900–1] 2001a: 175). The exploratory thinking and searching movement thus proposed also characterizes the phenomenological reading of anecdotes. This method, developed in the context of vignette and anecdote research (Schratz, Schwarz and Westfall-Greiter 2012: 38–41; Agostini and Peterlini 2022: 131), requires engaging with the text of an anecdote in its complexity and being open to different meanings to attribute to the verbal and bodily expressions described therein.

Reading the vignette is a process that involves repetition. Markus Ammann (2017a: 158), drawing from Paul Ricœur (1988), proposes two ways of reading. In a first 'innocent reading' (ibid.: 175), Ricœur is primarily concerned with 'aesthetic pleasure', which he distinguishes from 'mere satisfaction':

> Pleasure is a perceptive reception, attentive to the prescriptions of the musical score that the text is, one that opens up by virtue of the horizon aspect that Husserl attributed to all perception. By all these features, aesthetic perception is distinguished from everyday perception and thus establishes a distance in relation to ordinary experience. … The text first asks its readers to entrust themselves to this perceptive understanding, to the suggestions of meaning that a second reading will thematize, suggestions of meaning that will provide a horizon for this reading. (Ibid.: 174–5)

In this second reading, a reflective interpretation takes place from a more distanced and thus already emancipated stance from the first impression of the text. According to Ricœur, a third 'reading of verification' in the hermeneutic tradition would enable a comparison 'between the past horizon of the work and the present horizon of reading' (ibid.) and lead to a provisionally applicable result. In the phenomenological understanding, these ways of reading can also merge, and enjoyable reading and reflective viewing can replace one another without necessarily arriving at a final or clarifying judgment. The phenomenological interpretation thus leaves the hermeneutic three-step of understanding, explanation and application, as outlined by Ricœur in reference to Gadamer (ibid.: 174).

Evi Agostini (2016b) vividly describes the back and forth of phenomenological reading in the story 'Mr Palomar' by the writer Italo Calvino (1999). Palomar wants to acknowledge and explain the world correctly and through exact perception. However, the diversity, inscrutability and mysteriousness of the world thwart his investigations (Agostini 2016b: 55). When a wall, a mussel shell, a leaf or a teapot forces its way into his field of vision, his endeavours to leave his ego out of the equation ultimately fail: 'But how can you look at something and set your ego aside? Whose eyes are doing the looking?' (Calvino 1985: 114). Little by little, Mr Palomar discovers the connection between the thing observed and the observer, between the external and the internal, between the self and the world: 'The world is out there; and in here, what do we have? The world still – what else could there be?' (ibid.).

In terms of epistemology, Palomar thus casts doubt on the distinction between the perceiving subject and the perceived object, referred to in phenomenology as the difference between *noesis* (mode of access) and *noema* (factual content). The phenomenological conclusion from this is that we cannot observe, perceive or experience something as something *in and of itself*, but always only *something as something*, as derived from Husserl's statement that consciousness is always 'consciousness of something' (Husserl [1913] 2014: 169).

Therefore, what applies to the writing of the anecdotes also determines their reading. We do not decipher an absolute meaning independent of our perception by constantly attempting to relate to single passages in the text. Rather, a range of possible meanings is established in our perception. These are not detached from our own experiences. How we have perceived the person during the conversation if we have had it ourselves, and how the written text appeals to us (affects us) when we reread it, whether we have had similar or contrasting experiences of our own – all this goes into the constitution of meaning. Alternatively, to put it the other way around, our searching movements as readers in the text of the anecdote pass through our own experiences so that everything we can understand is equally enriched and contaminated by these experiences. Resonance reading does not produce neutral results but opens up possible ways of understanding. The way we look at the statements and descriptions in the anecdote, the contexts in which we can place them, the theoretical perspectives from which we read them and the personal experiences in the background make them appear to us *as something*. A multi-perspective way of reading will open up a variety of possible meanings.

Let us return to anecdote 2 (see 13) by Heike, who remembers the excursion to a former National Socialist concentration camp (Section 1.2).

> Heike has always been interested in history, and she had already been thinking about Mauthausen before the excursion. 'We were there now, and it was, it was, very intense', she whispers pensively, 'Are those still the cobblestones from that time?' Heike didn't expect them to be. 'It's hard to imagine what was there', she concludes, thoughtfully falling silent. (Ammann et al. 2017: 190)

In the anecdote, cobblestones play a mysterious role. What meanings can be inferred from reading this one passage? Taken literally, Heike only asks herself whether the cobblestones she saw in Mauthausen are those 'from that time'. In the reading process, a narrow understanding of the question could focus on the authenticity of the staging for the visitors. Based on this, a subject such as Holocaust denial, for example, could be addressed. Anyone who has already read something about Mauthausen will know that the concentration camp was built with walls made of granite stones that the prisoners themselves quarried nearby. Furthermore, anyone who has been to Mauthausen themselves or seen pictures will read the sentence in light of the experience of how massive, even oppressive, these granite walls can appear to onlookers. If we always perceive something as something, then we do not perceive a cobblestone itself but cobblestones as something. Cobblestones can be a functional building material. When laid on the ground, they make soft soil tread-proof; when piled up, they create walls or even just piles of stones. They can serve as projectiles with which to stone people. They can be used as hammers, for example, to drive wooden stakes into the ground or as a deadly weapon to strike someone's head.

The author of these lines was never in Mauthausen and did not recall any pictures of this camp when he read the anecdote. Nor did he interview Heike himself. When he first read this anecdote, he had nothing but the few lines of text that narrated Heike's remembered experiences. What approximations of the possible meanings of the cobblestones emerged in his first reading? Just the way Heike pensively whispers before asking whether those still are the cobblestones 'from that time' moved him, as if he had experienced something of the pupil's dismay while reading. For him, the question was simply an expression of bewilderment, of wordlessness in the face of the incomprehensibility of the Holocaust, as if Heike, trying to understand the incomprehensible, had to cling to something banal, to the question of whether those were the cobblestones from that time. In her famous report on the trial of Adolf Eichmann, Hannah Arendt ([1963] 2006) spoke of 'the banality of evil'. The German-Austrian officer of the SS-Schutzstaffel was one of the principal organizers of the Holocaust. He organized the transports to the camps, took care of the logistics, and routinely visited all the concentration camps to see how things were going and to check that the mass killings were functioning correctly. Even without reading Arendt, could Heike encounter this banality of evil in her recollection of these cobblestones and be struck by it? 'Heike', the anecdote tells us, 'didn't expect them to be' the original stones. And 'thoughtfully falling silent,' she concludes: 'It's hard to imagine what was there.' Right up to the present day, the Holocaust remains incomprehensible. Despite all the historical and analytical reappraisal, we are left with its silence, a lack of words, looking at a cobblestone without knowing what it means.

The previous paragraphs can serve as an example for the beginning of a resonance reading of Heike's anecdote, which at first glance is based solely on the engagement with what is described in the text, as the reader – the author of these lines – had nothing else at his disposal. Nevertheless, this reading is co-constituted by prior experiences and prior knowledge. His knowledge of the Holocaust – not of Mauthausen, but of other memorials of Nazi crimes – flows into the co-experience of what is expressed in the anecdote using Heike as an example. He has read Arendt and engaged with her hypothesis on the banality of evil. In empathizing with the anecdote, a web of meaning is woven: from the anecdote, he is affected by the description of Heike's bodily-verbal memory, her silence, her understandable incredulous gaze at the cobblestones, the association of wordless bewilderment. In reflection, the hypothesis of the banality of evil penetrates his consciousness from his own memory, as he sees it embodied in the astonishment and puzzlement over the cobblestones. It would also make sense for someone who had visited Mauthausen and knew about the connection between the often deadly work in the quarry and the construction of the concentration camp by its victims to read the story differently. Then, Heike's questioning gaze at the cobblestones would be mixed with images of the people who collapse to the ground in exhaustion in these quarries and despair in front of those stone walls. One could also reflect on how the monstrosity of the Holocaust feeds the doubts of those who cannot or do not want to believe it, suppressing the horror, guilt and shame. For the author of these lines, such a reading could only make sense insofar as Heike's question shows how easily the truth of the Holocaust could be called into question. Heike herself does not do this; her understandable, tangible consternation does not doubt but falls silent in the face of the undeniable. But those who want to sow doubt could plant it here: who is to say, a Holocaust denier might argue, that the Allies did not build these walls to falsely accuse Hitler's Germany of mass murder? The question of whether these were really the cobblestones of that time would then take on a completely different meaning. The anecdote about Heike does not allow this: in her silence, the fundamental phenomenological assumption is revealed that while we may not be able to uncover the essential truth of things, the things do indeed speak to us, and this speaking has something to do with a truth underlying things. The cobblestones tell the terrible story that still silences a schoolgirl almost a century later.

In the ongoing examination of the anecdote, we can see how further interpretations have also emerged without concluding the process of interpretation. Let us come back to Italo Calvino's fictional character. In his observation of the world, Mr Palomar makes another discovery fundamental to the phenomenological approach: 'It is only after you have come to know the surface of things', he believes, 'that you can venture to seek what is underneath. But the surface of things is in-exhaustible' (Calvino 1985: 55). The literary scholar Susan Sontag develops a similar idea for examining texts. Contrary to the trend in literary studies to explore a hidden meaning behind the texts when analysing them, she insists on simply remaining with the text itself, allowing herself to be touched by it:

> What is important now is to recover our senses. We must learn to see more, to hear more, to feel more. Our task is not to find the maximum amount of content in a work of art, much less to squeeze more content out of the work than is already there. Our task is to cut back content so that we can see the thing at all. (Sontag 1966: 10)

To arrive at the things themselves as they appear in our sensory perception, the eidetic reduction has been given a contemporary interpretation here.

6.2 'Pointing to' or 'pointing out'?

The phenomenological attitude of not looking for an essentialist reality behind things has a famous mentor. For the German writer Johann Wolfgang von Goethe, 'the ultimate goal would be to grasp that everything in the realm of facts is already theory. The blue of the sky reveals to us the basic law of chromatics. Let us not seek for something behind the phenomena – they themselves are the theory'[1] (Goethe [1810] 1988: 307). For Raab et al. (2008: 14), Goethe thus assumes that

> in a way, the phenomenological programme presented at the beginning of the 20th century anticipated this as well as an extremely important point of view for qualitative social research, which only became established several decades later. From a phenomenological point of view, it makes no sense to claim that there is something 'fundamental', 'actual' or 'essential' behind or beyond things, from which the concretely perceptible only provides a mere appearance and pale reflection. This is because individuals' understanding of themselves and reality, as well as the meanings they attach to their actions, are not hidden beneath

the phenomena but are perceptible to the senses in the symbolic and sign systems they use.

For Pessoa, 'things themselves are the only hidden meaning of things' (Pessoa 1989: 69). What does this mean for the concrete methodological application of reading anecdotes? The question touches on a crucial topic of phenomenological research, namely, the practical realization of a philosophical attitude towards the world and its phenomena. We encounter an ambivalence of openness and confusion. The phenomenological approaches are 'extraordinarily diverse in their interests, in their interpretation of the central issues of phenomenology, in their application of what they understood to be the phenomenological method, and in their development of what they took to be the phenomenological programme for the future of philosophy' (Moran 2000: 3). Thus, for Wertz (2005: 175), phenomenology is 'a low hovering, in-dwelling, meditative philosophy that glories in the concreteness of person-world relations and accords lived experience, with all its indeterminacy and ambiguity, primacy over the known'. As diverse as the resulting possibilities for research are, according to Finlay (2009: 7), they open up the constant 'spirited debate [about] how to do phenomenological research in practice'. This phenomenological openness can also cause uncertainty, mainly due to the lack of systematized and sequenced rules for the procedure, as to what one can orientate oneself on when hardly any concrete instructions are prescribed. Concerning Giorgi (1989), Finlay names four core characteristics of phenomenological research: 'The research is rigorously descriptive, uses the phenomenological reductions, explores the intentional relationship between persons and situations, and discloses the essences, or structures, of meaning immanent in human experiences through the use of imaginative variations' (Finlay 2009: 7).

As with other phenomenological approaches, this results in a need for clarification for anecdote research. Anecdotes arise from conversations in which people recall and describe experiences; at the same time, the anecdote includes descriptions of the situation, the course of the conversation and the interlocutors. But is this a rigorously pure description, or does it not inevitably also include interpretations? Roughly speaking, two orientations have emerged in the phenomenological history of ideas. On the one hand, there is strictly descriptive phenomenology, represented among others by Giorgi. Research oriented towards the latter attempts to use exemplary descriptions to demonstrate the meaning structures of a phenomenon with general significance. They remain close to the richness and complexity of the phenomenon and make statements based on an intuitive view and description of the phenomenon (see Finlay 2009: 11). In deviation from this, an 'interpretative phenomenology' (ibid.) has developed, particularly in the wake of Martin Heidegger and Hans Gadamer, which assumes an inescapable contingency of all human understanding due to the embedding of every perception – and consequently also description – in language, social contexts and world enmeshment; contemporary research in this direction includes, for example, the Interpretative Phenomenological Analysis of Smith (2004). In this perspective, interpretation is not separable from perception but intertwined with it: 'We experience a thing as something that has already been interpreted' (Finlay 2009: 11). The very fact that adjectives must be used for descriptions inevitably mixes them with interpretations.

Regardless of the different schools of thought, phenomenological research practice shows 'description and interpretation as continuum where specific work may be more or less interpretative' (ibid.). Thus, according to Langdridge, the boundaries between description and interpretation are also permeable. A rigid insistence on these boundaries 'would be antithetical to the spirit of the phenomenological tradition that prizes individuality and creativity' (Langdridge 2008: 1131).

For resonance reading of anecdotes, Gadamer's (1976: 11) double meaning of interpretation can be a helpful guideline. The German word for interpretation, *Deuten*, has an ambiguity, namely, on the one hand, simply *pointing to* something and, on the other hand, *pointing out* something in the sense of interpreting, as giving things a meaning. Based on the work of Finlay, the attitude of pointing to an 'interpretation suited to phenomenological description' (Finlay 2009: 11) was adopted for the resonance reading of anecdotes. In contrast with this is the 'interpretation as pointing out the meaning of something by imposing an external framework (such as when offering a psychoanalytic interpretation)' (ibid).

Consequently, there are two ways of interpreting anecdotes, the first of which corresponds to the phenomenological approach. In the sense of epistemological openness, the second way is also possible in principle. Thus, on the part of vignette and anecdote research, our data (vignettes and anecdotes) are always open to the empirical analysis of other epistemological approaches. The remembered experiences described and presented in the anecdotes would then be analysed from a psychoanalytical, constructivist, system-theoretical or ethnographic perspective. In this way, the phenomenological surplus would be made accessible to other approaches.

The two basic attitudes in reading, *pointing to* and *pointing out*, hardly exist in pure form. As much as phenomenological researchers may try to free themselves from presuppositions, they are inevitably guided in their *pointing to* by prior knowledge based on experience and theory. According to Gadamer ([1960] 1994), every new insight not only requires prior understanding but can be suitable for a better and deeper understanding of the phenomena we address if we 'have the courage to make use of your *own* understanding', as Gadamer (271) plays with Kant's famous maxim to make use of your own intellect. Gadamer's suggestions that this can happen primarily through dialogue between prior knowledge and text in terms of research methodology are methodologically adopted by Alvesson and Sandberg (2022): 'Key in this dialogue is to be able to identify productive aspects of our pre-understanding and to differentiate them from constraining aspects, thereby weeding out fixed ideas, confirmation bias and other blinders' (398). For them, it is not primarily about adhering to 'a strict methodological procedure …. Instead, it is about bringing our pre-understanding into a dialogical conversation with data and theory, in which they provoke each other in ways that open up and bring the phenomenon at issue into view' (ibid.).

Inspired by the steps of phenomenological reduction and Husserl's zigzagging, the following indications for the approach to reading the anecdotes can be summarized:

1. Read the anecdote attentively, even several times, preferably in the *pointing to* position:
  i. Pay particular attention to individual passages or words; what do these passages refer to that I already know?
  ii. What questions arise from individual passages or words about contexts that are new or unfamiliar to me?

2. Looking at the big picture again from the detail:
   i. Relate different passages or words in the text.
   ii. Recognize, separate and reconnect narrative structures.
3. Be guided by what particularly affects the anecdote:
   i. What do I notice?
   ii. What provokes me? What don't I understand?
   iii. What touches me emotionally (positively or negatively)?
4. Attention to physical and verbal speech in the anecdote:
   i. What manifests itself physically?
   ii. What is spoken verbally?
   iii. Do verbal and body expressions contradict or reinforce each other?
5. Read the passages that concern me the most again very carefully:
   i. Why might I have been affected by precisely these passages?
   ii. Did I read them accurately or inaccurately?
   iii. Did I read something inaccurately by quickly categorizing my assumptions?
6. Search for blind spots in the text:
   i. Have I read parts of the text only in passing or skipped over them?
   ii. Why did I ignore them or consider them unimportant?
   iii. What could be the meaning of these passages?
   iv. Have I read something in a single, familiar way, even though there are other ways of reading it?
7. Awareness and disclosure of occurring interpretations:
   i. Which interpretations of individual passages or even just words come to mind first?
   ii. Where do these interpretations come from?
   iii. Are they pleasant or do they disturb me?
   iv. Does this give rise to new questions?
8. Clarification of my prior knowledge and assumptions:
   i. What do the first interpretations that come to mind have to do with my previous knowledge?
   ii. What personal experiences do the experiences described in the anecdote relate to?

9. Variation of possible meanings:
    i. What other interpretations open up if I bracket my previous knowledge? Can I try to understand these passages or words in a completely different way than I was led to do on the basis of my previous assumptions or experiences?
10. Clarification of one's own theoretical 'spectacles':
    i. Which theories open up which perspectives on the anecdote?
    ii. Which of these are everyday theories, and which are academic theories?
11. Back to the text:
    i. What exactly does it say when I try to refrain from my theories and interpretations?
    ii. How do *pointing to* and *pointing out* relate to my research process?
12. Summarizing reading while preserving the diversity of meaning:
    i.   Which statements, descriptions and recalled experiences are significant for me?
    ii. Can these serve as examples for general findings?
    iii. What phenomena emerge in this anecdote?
    iv. How can I describe these phenomena by *pointing to* something in the anecdote?
    v.   Which theories can help me to better understand the phenomena shown in the anecdote?

Of course, this sketch of possible steps is not a sequenced procedure to work through entirely and in linear order. Phenomenological zigzagging means deviations from the path, detours and perhaps even shortcuts. In the foreground is the endeavour to maintain an attitude of openness, a renunciation of hasty categorization and definitive assertions in favour of varying possible meanings, weighing up more plausible interpretations against those that seem improbable to us but are not entirely impossible.

A unique feature of phenomenological reading is that it can lead to different results from different perspectives. Different readers will develop different ways of reading, which may complement each other, contrast or coexist but also exclude each other mutually (Agostini, Peterlini and Schratz 2019). In addition, every understanding is always provisional and never a complete process: the same anecdote read by the same person only a few weeks apart can open up different perspectives and ways of reading.

This openness does not mean scholarly arbitrariness but respect for the multifaceted nature of things that appear *as something*. This *something* shows aspects of the thing and the phenomenological surplus; it changes depending on the respective context in which the things appear to us, by their function in the respective context, by the temporal and spatial framing in which they appear to us, as well as by the position of the reader, who looks at the same thing with different potential means of understanding. To paraphrase Gadamer, 'To understand a text always means to apply it to ourselves and to know that, even if it must always be understood in different ways, it is still the same text presenting itself to us in these different ways' (Gadamer [1960] 1994: 416).

Based on these fundamental explanations, the method of reading should become more evident when it is concretized in the next chapter using different settings and illustrated with examples.

6.3 Settings of reading: Diving for phenomenological pearls

Reading and re-reading during the process of formulating, validating and finalizing the anecdote

An initial reading of the anecdotes already takes place during the writing process thereof. In the course of the narrative condensation of passages of conversation and the bodily expressions, the author of the anecdote herself reads it several times. She will visualize the conversational situation and check the coherence of her representation. In this phase, the reading is not yet used for evaluation but for fine-tuning the anecdote; inevitably, this intensive examination of one's own text already leads to reflections on the phenomena emerging from the text, and, at least unconsciously, the constitution of meaning is also likely to emerge. However, the focus is still on a description as close as possible to the co-experience of the conversation, while interpretations are avoided as much as possible. However, since the use of adjectives and the choice of words when describing a vocal expression (loud, shrill, energetic?) also implicitly represent interpretations, it is important in this phase not to think about the output of a possible interpretation for one's own research purpose but to continue to be affected by what is described and to remain close to the process of observing the conversation being edited.

The same applies to the next important step of intersubjective validation, as described in Section 5.4. The anecdote is subjected to intensive reading within the research group or with other *critical friends*, checked for discrepancies, cleared of anticipatory and explanatory interpretations and thus converted into a final version. In this process, too, decisions such as opting for a specific choice of wording, leaving a conversational situation open or intensifying or changing the punchline will presumably be implicitly linked to interpretations; once again, however, these are bracketed in favour of working on the raw version of the anecdote and its consistency with the conversation. If interpretations emerge in these phases of early reading, it can be helpful to make them transparent and note them down for the later phase of analysing the reading.

Dialogue reading – working in pairs

Dialogical or plurilogical reading occurs in an exchange between at least two readers or within a small research group or resonance community. Different creative realizations are possible for this approach. For example, a researcher can read their anecdote to a limited number of colleagues or persons with a specific professional background or present it for reading. For dialogue-based reading, it is advisable to stick to the anecdote and not reveal any context about how it came about, the biographies of the people described or other background information. The co-readers give feedback from their perspective on what they notice about the anecdote, what makes them wonder, what perturbs or affects them and what touches them positively or negatively. In this phase, the author of the anecdote takes on the role of the listener. In this way, the author receives feedback and points of view that he or she would perhaps never have received – through the knowledge of the context, the conduction of the conversation and the already advanced processes of interpretation. These could also be factually misleading interpretations or at least ones that seem utterly absurd to the author. Nevertheless, even such *false* or *absurd* interpretations have a meaning in the conventional discourse on truth. They reveal ways of thinking and perceiving that would never have occurred to the author of the anecdote and thus broaden her or his perspectives. Precisely because the dialogue partners have no background knowledge and no context for the anecdote, they do not move within the author's categories of thought and thwart their existing interpretations, be they unconsciously or consciously formed. The author may accept some things as an extension of their own perceptual horizon and reject others. However, even from those interpretations which do not resonate with the author, she or he will have experienced and learned something about perspectives on her anecdote. The reader may recognize additional or slightly altered phenomena in the vignette that would have escaped the author's attention, which now lead her or him down new paths or open up a more reflective view. After a certain saturation of interpretations – this usually occurs after twenty minutes – the author of the anecdote can now present their own point of view in about ten minutes and discuss it with the co-reader; this also includes the author of the vignette providing feedback on how their own perception has been enriched or challenged. This way, the co-reader learns more about the anecdote and gains broader perspectives. It is of particular importance if the co-reader is an addressee of the research, such as a teacher, school principal or even an educational planner, insofar as it concerns anecdotes about learning processes, school experiences and educational biographies. It could also be a reading of a patient's anecdote about her hospitalization (with healthcare professionals), a young person in care (with a youth service professional) or the residents of a suburban housing estate (with a town planner or urban safety officer). Engaging with the anecdote and the author's feedback stimulates professional reflexivity and expands specialized knowledge beyond the usual familiar approaches.

    The interpretations of the dialogue partners do not have to converge in the end; different understandings can remain. The important thing is that there has been a dialogue and an exchange of different perspectives on the surplus contained in the anecdote – the phenomenological treasure trove.

Plurilogical reading – working in groups

Reading in groups is characterized by a similar approach to dialogue reading. The most crucial difference is the larger setting, which increases the possibilities of divergent, complementary or even contrasting perspectives due to the more significant number of participants. A well-thought-out framework is helpful for this. In workshops with significantly more than ten to fifteen participants, it can be helpful to form subgroups that take turns in the interpretation process. This way, about fifteen participants might participate intensively in the group reading of the first anecdote, while the other thirty initially only act as listeners. In the next round, with a new anecdote, it is group B's turn and, finally, group C's. A good hour should be allowed to discuss one anecdote, as thinking back and forth in a larger group requires a prolonged exploratory phase and only gradually becomes more in-depth. It would be a pity to stop because time is running out. Depending on the setting, it is advisable to allow ninety minutes, including a break, for each anecdote.

The experiences with group reading are varied. One possibility is to offer anecdotes related to the respective field of expertise during workshops on professional development and training. The setting requires a clear introduction and structure. It is advisable to form a seating circle, as hierarchies are less prominent in such a setting, and everyone speaks to everyone else, whereas frontal arrangements reinforce hierarchies. The introduction should include making the aim and purpose of the meeting or workshop transparent and, if the group is unfamiliar with anecdote research, briefly outlining this. This phase does not require meticulous details; the basic idea is sufficient, that is, that these are anecdotes from conversations with those affected and involved from a specific target group. It is not about objective truths but rather subjective memories and intersubjective interpretations. It is also important to point out that it is not a question of finding the *one* correct meaning but of engaging with the anecdote and being open to a variety of possible interpretations.

When choosing anecdotes for such a setting, there are, in principle, two possibilities – that of a confrontation and that of an exemplary discussion. What is meant by this? If we are talking about a teachers' meeting at a particular school, the confrontational approach would involve confronting the teachers with anecdotes from their pupils or school dropouts or with stories from teachers from that school expressing frustration about developments in the teaching profession and the increasing bureaucratic pressure. The anecdotes would relate directly to the participants, and the readers would be co-affected. The problems of such an approach are apparent: the reading could cause embarrassment, defensive attitudes or even attempts to refute or prove the lived experiences recalled in the anecdote. Instead of an open exploration that welcomes different interpretations, there could be a division into camps because one part of the group backs up the circumstances addressed in the anecdote while the other refutes them. Furthermore, the details of the story could hardly protect the anonymity of the participants in the anecdote. Such an approach is, as best, possible within a group with a high degree of critical faculties, frustration tolerance, solidarity and trust between everyone. The researcher must be clear that it is not about strengthening one's position at the expense of others and that one's own interests are not at risk; rather, it is only about the team learning together from cases already known to everyone. Similarly, there should be no hierarchical differences in the team, such as the presence of a school principal, when it comes to cases that affect teachers at this school. Under these conditions, the confrontational approach could be helpful because the anecdotes are directly related to the readers, and they thus gain broader perspectives on their immediate field of work.

In most cases, however, a confrontational approach is not recommended. Methodologically and epistemologically, it is also not recommended because phenomenological research is not about debating one's direct reality but about learning via examples, which can stand for a universally valid reality. A familiar experience with plurilogical group (as well as dialogical) reading is that participants are much more open to an anecdote if they are not personally involved in its background. From this safe position, they can better recognize and accept the patterns of their profession and actions from the content of the anecdote they are unfamiliar with. In such reading workshops, it is common to hear calls such as 'this could be my own teaching', 'this looks so familiar to me' or 'the person in this anecdote could be me'. It is precisely because the anecdote does not concern them personally that a protected space for discourse and thought is created, which facilitates free exploration and promotes the recognition of one's own – similar or different – experiences and patterns.

Let us describe the procedure using the example of a seminar group as part of a university degree programme. The course leader introduced the participants to anecdote research in the first seminar. Then everyone conducts an interview or intensive conversation as homework, which is related to the seminar topic in the broadest sense; it is also permissible to use impromptu conversations that arise by chance. The participants each write an anecdote from this material. In the remaining class sessions, the anecdotes are read together in plenary. Each anecdote reading needs approximately one hour. The anecdote is projected onto the screen using a projector and read aloud by the author. A joint reading follows this phase while the author stands back and listens. The moderator of the reading, usually the seminar leader, asks the participants to spontaneously give feedback on what they notice, what makes them hesitate and what particularly affects them. In the first phase, the facilitator asks them not to make hasty interpretations or decipher the meaning of the anecdote or individual passages but to point out what is described in the anecdote and how. After a certain amount of saturation, usually after about twenty minutes, the possibilities for attempting interpretations are pointed out. Everything is allowed; nothing has to be correct, and nothing can be wrong. Gradually, different facets or aspects of one or more phenomena emerge from this process. The moderator engages with the individual interpretations offered and, if possible, links them to possible theories or conceptual models that support such a viewpoint or that would be strengthened or relativized by such an interpretation. As shown in the dialogue setting, the result is a kind of tapestry of meaning with colourful patterns and many links and also open spaces, unclear spots, cracks and considerations that do not fit together. All of this can be left as it is. When saturation becomes apparent in this phase, too, usually after another twenty minutes, the author of the anecdote gets the floor. The author can respond to the feedback, compare their own perceptions and add context. This feedback is usually preceded by statements about how grateful they are to have been offered so many interpretations that would never have occurred to them. Their understanding, limited to a particular point of view by prior assumptions and contextual knowledge, has now been enriched. Even interpretations that seem wrong based on background knowledge will have opened up new perspectives that help to broaden one's views and recognize new options for action. In a short final round, the plenary can reflect on the process once again, and the moderator can also comment on the process from their perspective and, if necessary, point out helpful theories and models to delve deeper into the topics discussed. As in the entire setting, methodological and epistemological information on the phenomenological approach is provided at appropriate points. In the case of an academic seminar group, this includes the author of the anecdote writing a scholarly reading text (see section 'Resonance reading as an academic text' in this chapter).

Such an approach is possible with participants from all disciplines, including empirical or other propositional studies, as well as with different professional groups. If it would be inappropriate or too cumbersome and time-consuming for students or professionals to create anecdotes from their own interviews, this step can be skipped. In this case, the setting would be less of an introduction to the method and testing it and more of a reflection workshop to gain a more refined perception of essential topics for one's area of interest and to understand them from a broader perspective.

Scenic reading – empathize with the actors of an anecdote

Scenic reading of vignettes and anecdotes (Peterlini 2017: 52) was first developed as a methodological extension during a seminar with students reading a vignette. It described a heated argument between two pupils in a school class. In order to avoid violence, the teacher stepped between the two pupils and restrained one of them by pressing his hand roughly against his chest (ibid.: 50). When reflecting on the vignette, a contentious discussion arose about whether such physical intervention was necessary or an assault. A polemic pro and con debate ensued, making exploring the possible interpretations almost impossible. At this point, the seminar leader suggested acting out the scene. Elements of interactive forum theatre (see Boal 1993) were spontaneously used to let different students take turns acting out the scene. After the short performances, the students told how they felt about the grab on the chest. Gradually, various accounts emerged of how the aggression between the students and the teacher's intervention felt. The previously contentious debate, which amounted to a true–false dichotomy, was enriched by many intermediate perceptions and ambivalent interpretations that could coexist as different perspectives and aspects of the same phenomenon (Peterlini 2017: 52–4).

Scenic reading as an interpretative method of vignette and anecdote research has since found further applications, for instance, at the 4th International Symposium on Phenomenological Educational Science, which took place at the Humboldt University Berlin in September 2017 under the title 'Leib – Leiblichkeit – Embodiment' (Agostini et al. 2019). The vignette used was about the student Kristin, who stands at the blackboard in maths class and repeatedly comes to a standstill in her calculation process, puts the chalk down, lowers her hand again, presses it against her thigh and waits for the teacher to help her, who finally solves the problem for her. When the teacher asks her if she has understood everything, she nods silently, puts the chalk down and returns to her seat (ibid.: 204–5).

At the symposium, the audience was asked to pantomime the pupil's movements in order to empathize with her. The interpretations were again varied, sometimes even contradictory. While some saw the scene on the blackboard as an expression of powerlessness, for others, Kristin skilfully used her helplessness to get help. A debate arose in the plenary session as to whether, in terms of plausibility, two such opposing interpretations are possible and whether it is not necessary to decide in favour of one – either feigned helplessness or actual powerlessness. In the written contribution to this scenic reading, the authors write, 'How Kristin really feels at the blackboard, whether her gestures and postures indicate a feeling of failure or a searching hesitation that challenges the teacher to help and thus helps her out of a lack of preparation, could not be answered even if Kristin were asked about it immediately after the event' (ibid.: 210). The bodily expression can also consist in the staging of ambivalence, the ambiguity between not being able to, not wanting to and not trusting oneself, especially in a situation of performance challenge under the gaze of the teacher and the entire class. The controversial feedback from the plenary expressed this ambiguity.

Another example is the following reading of an episode in a school class with young refugees. The scenic sequence, intended initially as a vignette, corresponds to an anecdote by including an impromptu conversation between the researcher and the pupil Rashed.

Anecdote 11

In creative lessons, one group of young refugees is given the task by Ms Bauer to finish painting their 'broken cities', and a second group gets the task of finishing their 'beautiful cities'. The groups are spatially separated. I follow the group with the task about broken cities. Rashed realizes, as his hasty turning around suggests, that I am walking behind him and suddenly says to me quietly: 'I don't know why I am in the group with the broken cities. Ms Bauer did not allow me to go in the group with the beautiful cities.' He shrugs his shoulders and shakes his head. Sighing, he says, 'I'd rather be in the group with the beautiful cities.' Once in the classroom, two children unpack their brushes and paints. Rashed carefully takes some pens out of the box and concentrates on drawing a building, flames and people with machine guns. When he sees I am watching him paint, he tells me: 'There are beautiful cities in Afghanistan, but I have to paint a broken city.' With a frown and a tight face, he looks at his picture and takes the yellow pencil to colour the flames an even brighter yellow. (Lehner and Peterlini 2020: 94)

The episode takes place in the present and yet bears traces of the memory of Rashed's country of origin. In a workshop at the symposium on vignette and anecdote research in Innsbruck, 'Understanding Experiences – Experiencing (Non-) Understanding' (29–31 August 2019), the participants were asked to stage the passages that particularly touched them in the room.[2] They adopted different postures and traced micro-movements as described in the vignette. The participants then shared their experiences, some verbally and some in writing. For example, the shrugging of the shoulders and the quick turn were perceived as particularly impactful gestures and interpreted as a protest, as if Rashed wanted to emphasize what he had expressed verbally in a rather cautious manner, as if he were saying much more clearly with his body: 'I am not one of those who live in broken cities.' The turning towards the researcher walking behind him was interpreted as resistance: 'I'm looking for help and I'm sharing myself.' Shrugging his shoulders was re-experienced both as a gesture of shaking off his anger and as an expression of incomprehension. For the participants, the vigorous colouring was a sign of the pressure that had been exerted on him and, at the same time, of the strength that he was exerting against this pressure. It was disconcerting to see Rashed carefully pick up the pencil and then paint an inferno. Resistance can also manifest itself in the execution of orders with exaggerated vigour. Thus, bodily protest is evident, which only restrained on a verbal level (Lehner and Peterlini 2020: 94–5). Methodologically, this intervention shows how scenic reading creates spaces for differentiations and reambiguations of attributions and discriminatory categorizations. The participants in the symposium were able to empathize with and experience Rashed's dilemma through scenic empathy. By empathizing with micro-sequences of the vignette, it also became physically perceptible how it feels to be subjected to stereotyping.

The method of scenic reading used so far, mainly for vignettes, is analogically well suited for anecdotes. Let us take again the example of the anecdote about Heike in Mauthausen. The questions raised by her reflections on the cobblestones there indeed invite a scenic reading. How does it feel when we repeat her sentence and look at these cobblestones in our minds: 'We were there now, and it was, it was, very intense', she whispers pensively, 'Are those still the cobblestones from that time?'

Meyer-Drawe recognizes the excellent potential for phenomenological research in scenic empathy: 'It is immediately obvious that the sensuality of experience is essential in such productions. Now you really can raise your fist, pluck at the hem of your jumper, brush your hair behind your ear, squint your eyes, raise your voice, express shame or anger, pierce the tabletop with your gaze, yawn, grin …, clear your throat and more' (Meyer-Drawe 2020: 17). The descriptions of how something is spoken in an anecdote, the gestures and body postures that accompany the spoken content and the pitch and volume the speech become even more prominent in a scenic reading: 'Yet it is something else, for example, when I cough with gestural commentary, or when my cold causes these noises. These nuances are difficult to capture solely linguistically' (ibid.). Through empathizing and bodily resonance, what is silenced linguistically is posed as a question to one's corporeality. According to Meyer-Drawe, the ability to physically experience something described by another person through bodily enactment, based on a text, is related to the bodily phenomenological understanding of intercorporeality. However foreign the other person may be to us, 'inter-bodily configurations, such as an affected silence, soothing or defensive touches or intersecting glances, can nonetheless be empathized with based on personal experience' (ibid.: 18).

Resonance reading as an academic text

As an instrument of structured research, the resonance reading of anecdotes also results in an academic text form. The reading settings presented here have a meaning in themselves but can also be combined; furthermore, they can be the first steps towards an academic text. In this way, implicit interpretations from the intersubjective validation can be taken into an explicit reading and revisited in a dialogical or group reading. Dialogical or group reading can encourage a scenic reappraisal of an anecdote or individual bodily expressions. The creation of the scholarly reading text is, after previous steps, usually a personal writing process in which the author revisits the anecdote from their own perspective and develops her findings from it.

The intensive re-reading of the anecdote required for this goes hand in hand with the written recording and argumentative presentation of the possible meanings. This process can be imagined in such a way that the researcher has the anecdote in front of them as a text, reads it several times, memorizes individual passages and lets them sink in. Earlier interpretations from previous readings in the research group can be incorporated, but the author's findings now take precedence.

In the next section, resonance reading as an academic text is presented using the example of a research project in which several research group members reflected on the same anecdote:

Anecdote 12

'By learning, you usually mean school performance, but something like friendship and so on, I learned that at school, too, and also in my free time', says Brigitta in the fourth grade, looking back. She raves about the 'best class' in which everyone gets along well, about the activities with friends from the class – and about Bianca. Bianca was new in the second grade, and Brigitta got along so well with her from the very first day. She never argued with her and they always helped each other with their studies. 'I often talk to her on the phone and do maths at the same time. She does maths, I do maths, and then', Brigitta laughs with amusement at the idea: 'over the cell phone.' She loves competitions in maths too. Actually, all subjects are fun with Bianca. 'She's always doing something, and she often laughs a lot', Brigitta describes her classmate dreamily. She thinks for a moment: 'We've all always got along well. But Bianca ...' she falters again, 'I don't know, but somehow ...' and after a short hesitation she continues: 'She had become my best friend' and 'that Bianca came to our class', Brigitta calls the most pleasing event of her entire time at this school. She smiles a bit bashfully and beams blissfully.[3] (Ammann, Westfall-Greiter and Schratz 2017: 165)

Six readings – by Gabriele Rathgeb, Michael Schratz, Veronika Möltner, Verena Leitner-Klaunzer, Silvia Krenn and Markus Ammann – were also published as part of the scholarly output of the project (Ammann, Westfall-Greiter and Schratz 2017: 165–86). For illustration, we will reprint two resonance readings in the next section in full and include another one for reflection as 'Reading the readings'.

Resonance reading 1: Friendship as competence (Rathgeb 2017: 167–8)

'By learning, you usually mean school performance, but something like friendship and stuff, I learned that at school, too.' Brigitta understands learning to mean more than just school performance. As a 13-year-old, she realizes that you can also learn other things. That seems extraordinary. The answers of most pupils to the question of what they had learned in the four years at the new secondary school confirm Brigitta's assumption regarding the usual understanding of learning: it is all about academic performance, knowledge and skills.

The statement, 'something like friendship and so on' indicates that there is more to enumerate here. Getting along with others, communicating, listening, resolving conflicts ... – This is perhaps how 'and so on' could be concretized. According to Brigitta, this learning also takes place in informal settings ('and also in my free time'), but not only there. Brigitta's statements suggest that she experiences school as a (living) space where she acquires social skills. The extent to which this is promoted and thematized by teachers or lessons remains open.

Can friendship be 'learned' at all? Brigitta's statement that she (also) learned 'friendship and so on' at school reflects a development in education and school policy. On the one hand, it implies that learning involves more than just acquiring knowledge. However, the expansion of the learning concept is not really new due to the paradigm shift in education policy that has taken place over the last decade. Educationalists and dieticians such as Heinrich Roth (1971) and Wolfgang Klafki (2007) were already including social, subject and personal competencies, long before the current debate on competence orientation. What is new is the idea that pupils can achieve these competencies in a targeted manner, possibly through a sophisticated didactic training plan, and that their success or failure in their achievement is testable. This optimism about testing and training fundamentally applies to all areas of human life. The message of proponents of this idea is that everything can be learned and trained. Anyone who wants to achieve something in this world has learned to manage themselves, their emotions and even their life, and to constantly optimize and adapt to changing requirements (Gelhard 2012). As schools are supposed to equip children and young people with the required skills, 'friendship and stuff' is also learned at school. Nobody would object to children and young people acquiring social skills at school. What requires critical debate is the tendency to categorize personal and social skills – including emotions, attitudes and behaviour – as trainable and testable. It was then possible to organize, manage and control friendships. Anyone who fails at this, who finds it difficult to make friends or maintain friendships over a more extended period, should complete further friendship training sessions. The test and training optimists promise that then it will definitely work out. This optimism does not consider the 'milieu- and everyday life-specific circumstances' (Meyer-Drawe 2012b: 33) of children and young people. The achievement, or lack thereof, of learning goals or competencies is considered a personal success or failure, regardless of their social background, gender or parents' educational background.

In addition, the idea of the feasibility of relationships fits very well into the concept of a neoliberal market economy. Among other things, friendships and relationships become a vehicle for promoting one's career and success. To be equipped for the demands of the free market, students should acquire relationship skills. 'Networking' is a central foundation for individual success.

To avoid misunderstandings, this is not to imply that Brigitta has her 'marketability' in mind when she raves about her friendship with Bianca. However, the wording Brigitta uses in this context is telling. It would probably never have occurred to 13-year-olds of the generation of the 1950s to talk about having *learned* friendship, especially at school. This paradigm shift in the concept of learning at school in the wake of educational standards and competence orientation is a new phenomenon. It seems to have arrived at school and apparently also among the pupils.

Resonance reading 2: School is more than the sum of teaching (Schratz 2017: 169–71)

What a school achieves is more than the sum of the lessons it provides – as the anecdote suggests. How does the individual school, as a sub-organizational unit of a systemic whole, an education system, manage to 'produce' responsible citizens as an 'output' in line with the national curriculum specifications and enable them to participate in social processes to shape a desirable future for the next generations? Is the administrative constitution of the location reflected in the implementation of school organization and teaching laws, making the necessary structural conditions for the design of successful educational processes possible? Is it the interplay between agency and structure, which Giddens (1997) emphasizes in his theory of structuring as constitutive for the connection between the individual and society? According to this theory, individuals act in and according to structures, while simultaneously creating new structural conditions through their actions. The new secondary school provided Brigitta with a space of experience that structurally opened up opportunities for her to develop pleasure and achievement but also made it a living space for her personal development and professional qualification. Bianca's entry into the classroom was a special kind of experience for Brigitta, a *Widerfahrnis*[4] (Meyer-Drawe 2008) that still causes her to falter when she talks about it. This event created space for a friendly bond, which for her was not only 'the most gratifying event of her entire time at school', but both girls cultivated this friendship in such a way that the school became a place for educational experiences in which they physically experienced the effectiveness of school curricula on and in themselves. For example, practising and cultivating a social interaction with each other ('She never argued with her and they always helped each other'), studying the subjects (especially maths) and the bodily experience of different learning arrangements (peer learning, meaningful practice, maths competition, multi-media learning) that achieves a kind of highest connection in the learning relationship in the synchronicity of 'She does maths, I do maths, and then.' The openness of the sentence indicates incompleteness and allows for perspective.

Is it the performance of those responsible for the school as an educational institution that enables pupils like Brigitta to experience successful educational processes? Is it the achievement of the school management, who may only have an indirect influence on the lessons but can do a lot to ensure that the school is more than just a place of learning, that it becomes a living space for a large part of the day, where young people are empowered to shape their own lives and life in society in a responsible and self-determined way? That there is 'time to grow, to mature, time to play, to learn, to be eager, to argue, to carry oneself, to rejoice, to mourn, to laugh, to cry, to feel, time to grow up and outgrow oneself, in confrontation and cooperation with others', as it says in the school programme of the Barmen (D) comprehensive school (Schratz 2015: 28).

For Brigitta, the performance of the school is reflected in the microcosm of the class in which she spent four years of her life and, looking back, causes her to gush: she raves about 'her class' as 'the best' in which everyone gets along well. Does her retrospection reveal the longing for the 'best' as an essential anthropological figure of human endeavour, or is it the retrospective glorification of past times?

In retrospect, the school class appears as an ecological context (οἶκος), as the micropolitical home of school interaction. From the shadow of her classmates, who all get on well but do not appear as people in the anecdote, her friends, particularly Bianca, stand out in her retrospective. Since she joined the class, she seems to have become the relevant other in many respects. It was a special moment for Brigitta, perhaps a magical one when Bianca entered her life in the second grade. She also assigns the attribute 'best' to her as a friend, as she has become this for Brigitte.

Such experiences cannot be planned, as they occur unexpectedly and bring something new into the world. They are life experiences: 'Even a small incident in a child's life is an experience of its lifeworld. For the child, therefore, it is an experience of the world' (Bachelard 1990: 33). As Brigitta's retrospective suggests, school is successful when it can open up new relationships to the world for learners in terms of content and socialization into which they can grow. Under what conditions and in what form can such a dialogue be realized? This is one of the tasks that schools have to solve if education and community are to become effective as the basis for responsible participation in sustainable social development.

The atmosphere supporting such a claim does not arise by itself; it is subject to the interplay between *agency* and *structure* presented above, which is exemplified in the school programme of the Barmen Comprehensive School as follows: 'The respective characteristics of space, architecture, tempo, dynamics, noise, rhythm, harmony, encounter, mood, feeling, climate, attitude characterize the atmosphere ... It is the perceptions of the other person that become visible to us when we engage with the other person in an open, empathetic and curious way. The way we encounter others has a strong influence on the atmosphere of our school' (Schratz 2015: 31).

In the four years of lower secondary school, the new secondary school created a space of experience for Brigitta that provided a supportive atmosphere for the 'best' encounters between her and the other classmates as well as between her and the subject matter, the specialized lessons, especially with Bianca and in the acquisition of mathematical knowledge, particularly emphasized in the anecdote. What the teachers contribute to this and what structures support the times and spaces for optimal learning and working are left out. However, they are part of creating such conditions that as *many* pupils as possible experience their school as 'the best'.

Reading the readings

The two texts seem to stand in stark contrast, although both are orientated towards the portrayal of Brigitta's story about her school and her friendship with Bianca. During the reading process, Gabriele Rathgeb was particularly struck by the fact that Brigitta seems to portray the learning of friendship as learning at school. For her, Brigitta's statement is caught up in the maelstrom of the discourse on competence, according to which everything can be learned with proper training and suitable methods, even friendship. In reflecting on the anecdote, this results in a criticism not of Brigitta but of such an education of mastery, according to which everything becomes controllable, didactically instructable and steerable. Michael Schratz is affected by the girl's enthusiasm for her school, where relationships can grow and, with Bianca's entry into the school as an utterly uncontrollable event, blossom into 'best' friendship. He sees this as an example of a school that stands in contrast to the discourses of competence criticized by Rathgeb, like an ecological *oikos*, an oasis where the interaction of agency and structure enables learning in a broad sense as learning and experiencing the world.

Who is right? Both or neither. The two researchers, colleagues in the same research group, allowed themselves to be addressed differently by the anecdote; they were touched by different aspects and were put on different tracks for their reflections on educational processes, structures and discourses. By engaging with the anecdote, they picked up on traces of the phenomenological surplus and developed them into academic considerations. For Rathgeb and Schratz, the multifaceted meaning of things has encountered different horizons of their own experience and has opened up different ways of thinking and possibilities of interpretation.

In her reading, the author of the anecdote, Silvia Krenn, adds an exciting aspect (Krenn 2017a: 222–6; 2017b). She addresses a fact that does not even appear in the anecdote. Bianca comes from Poland and did not speak a word of German when she started school, the moment which Brigitta describes as so magical. The mutual emotion between the girls apparently effortlessly overcame the linguistic and origin-related otherness. Indeed, for Brigitta as the main character, Bianca's origin was not worth mentioning in the intense, long conversation at the heart of the anecdote. This detail (not mentioned by Brigitta but added by the researcher in her reading) raises the methodological query of how to deal with contextual knowledge if it exists and is known. Ultimately, this question leads us to the threshold between phenomenological learning *by example* and hermeneutic learning by *case history* (see Agostini 2020). The exploration of context opens up the reconstructive path of case studies, in which exemplary life stories or learning biographies, for example, are illuminated as comprehensively as possible to conclude general contexts. The phenomenological limitation of staying with *what* shows itself endeavours to explore phenomena *by example*. In this approach, the aim is not to know more *about* Bianca's origins and her migration history but to understand something about friendship, relationships and learning in and out of school *from* Brigitta's story about Bianca. Both paths are academically challenging and potentially insightful; both touch on each other, intersect and sometimes coincide. It is, therefore, not a question of playing off one approach against the other but instead of demonstrating the different approaches to become aware of the methodological approach.

In this case, the author of the anecdote was aware of the context. Methodologically, she correctly refrained from including this in the anecdote, as it was not about her research but about Brigitta's remembered experiences. However, in reading and reflecting on the anecdote, she could not deny this knowledge. It is as much a part of her prior knowledge as Michael Schratz's knowledge of the repeatedly cited model secondary school in Germany. In reading, any prior knowledge and thus also any known context can be made transparent, helpful for, on the one hand, questioning one's own knowledge and prior experiences anew in the attitude of *pointing to* the descriptions in the anecdote and, on the other hand, using this own tool of perception to evoke interesting constitutions of meaning. Any prior knowledge, any contextual knowledge and any theoretical baggage helps to shape the reading, guides it and, at the same time, promotes new possibilities of interpretation. The author of the anecdote used the reading to enrich the example of this friendship for phenomenological exploration with a crucial detail, which opened new ways of understanding the magic encounter between the girls and allowed reflection about a friendship beyond the borders of language and cultural origin. It is important not to lapse into definitive assertions based on contextual knowledge or previous experience as to how the story is to be understood solely and exclusively but to offer these to the readers of the reading as a possible point of view. In her reading text, Silvia Krenn leaves it open as to what the migration story means for the friendship because, phenomenologically, it is not the causal justification of a phenomenon that is of interest but its appearance as it shows itself in the remembered experiences, without being able to be comprehensively explained in this way:

> A special friendship has developed here without being planned or caused. Brigitta can look back on it with enrichment and happiness. This experience seems to have had a powerful effect on her, modifying her world view and her relationship to herself and others. The experience of 'true friendship' gives her self-confidence, stability, and confidence in herself and others and strengthens her openness to new things. The future will show whether and how Brigitta processes her experience that not everything can be rationally justified. (Krenn 2017b: 183)

Phenomenological reading does not follow linear paths. It is a searching reading that is guided and shaped by the resonance between the reader and the text of the anecdote, that rubs against the fractures between the reader's own experience and that of the anecdote, that resists specific definitions and opens up spaces for further interpretations.

Notes

1. Goethe's aphorism can be translated from German in different ways. 'Phenomena' (originally *'Phänomene'*) sometimes are translated as 'appearances' or even 'things', and 'theory' (originally *'Lehre'*) can also be found as 'teaching' or even 'mystery'. The translation of Douglas Miller is preferred by Iris Hennigfeld (2015: 143) in her excellent essay 'Goethe's Phenomenological Way of Thinking and the Urphänomen' in the Goethe Yearbook. It seems the most suitable for this context.
2. The following comments on this scenic reading are taken from Lehner and Peterlini 2020: 95–9, translated by the authors.
3. Anecdote from the research project 'Personale Bildungsprozesse in heterogenen Gruppen. Langzeitstudie' (Lead Michael Schratz, funded by FWF P225373-G16).
4. The term *Widerfahrnis* underlines the passive aspect of experiences. Experiences in this meaning happen to us; we cannot control or even do them actively. It is mainly shaped by Bernhard Waldenfels (2007b: 45) in phenomenological philosophy and discussed intensively for educational aspects by Meyer-Drawe (2008). Norm Friesen (2014: 72) explains the term this way:

> This term begins with a prepositional prefix (*wider*) meaning 'against'; this is followed by the verb for experience, '*fahren*', to travel (with *erfahren* meaning to experience). The word ends, finally, with a substantivizing suffix, '-nis'. Together, these meanings suggest the kind of 'friction' that is inherent in all experience. It arises not from one's own action, but precisely through one's *passivity*. It is 'experience despite oneself' and 'against the grain', so to speak. It is a specific happening which jolts us, is negative, shakes us up, rattles us. Something drives (*fahren*) against us, so to speak, rather than just toward us. And as these characterizations suggest, the 'event', the encounter with the alien, is not something that occurs only sporadically, but is ongoing, a part of every event: 'Everything that happens to us, right up to the limit events of birth and death which are repeated in our life in different ways, may be called *pathos*, which is to be understood as what in German is called *Widerfahrnis*' (2007b: 45).

It should be added that *Widerfahrnis* could also be an overwhelmingly positive experience as the encounter between Brigitta and Bianca shows in the anecdote.

PART III

Potentials of anecdote research and outlook

CHAPTER 7

Examples of applications in different research fields and contexts

Anecdote research, like vignette research, was initially developed for research into learning processes at school that manifest themselves in the present through reminiscent speech and refer to meaningful earlier experiences. In addition to vignette research focusing on learning *in statu nascendi*, it should also be possible to trace learning and educational experiences in the past. Just as there have been further developments in vignette research that make it applicable to the reflection of learning processes and pedagogical action in other professional contexts and other public social spaces and institutions, the scope of application of anecdote research has also gradually expanded. This chapter offers examples of possible applications in school and education, ethnographic research in the humanities and social sciences, and biography and identity research. Finally, we propose and discuss anecdotes as a reflection tool for professional and organizational and professional development in different contexts.

7.1 Anecdotes as an approach to research in learning and teaching in schools

Anecdote 13

Brigitta's face lights up: 'The project in fourth-grade biology class was something very special for me', she says. She had to work on a topic independently and chose the human skeleton. 'I got an "excellent"' – Brigitta laughs amusedly – 'very good' and admits, 'I was really proud of that because I invested a lot of time in it. She adds happily: 'And I wrote everything by hand, and that was eighteen pages!' (Ammann et al. 2017: 190)

Anecdote 14

When asked about the best experience of his four years at secondary school, Leo cannot think of anything. Even asking several times does not change this. He cannot think of anything, he muses. 'And if you imagine you are an electrician and you think back to secondary school, what do you probably remember?' asks the researcher. To which Leo explains firmly: 'Yes, the best thing is that I will have finished school, just the four years, that I will go to poly',[1] and his eyes light up. (Ibid.: 193)

Both anecdotes come from the collection of the Innsbruck research group, which developed and first tested the method. In both anecdotes, children's eyes light up, but Leo's eyes light up for a completely different reason than Brigitta's. Brigitta remembers an experience of learning at school that gripped her and still lingers in the anecdote. On the one hand, Brigitta is still noticeably proud that she received an exceptional grade, namely an 'excellent very good'. There is no such mark in the Austrian grading scale, which Brigitta also makes clear with her amused way of speaking, but the wording expresses that it was not just one banal grade out of many but something extraordinary. For Brigitta, the 'very special' thing about the grade is the experience of a project lesson in which she was allowed to choose the topic herself and 'work on it independently'.

She explains her pride in the grade by saying she had invested 'a lot of time'. This shows a satisfaction that does not stem from formal aspects of school learning but from the experience of her very own achievement, which surprised her and opened up her potential and self-efficacy. The fact that she wrote eighteen pages by hand makes her happy. Her gratification about that shows the haptic aspect of achievement, which not only originated in the head but also involved the hand and thus the whole body. The recall is not tied only to the grade as proof of performance but also stored in the body's memory, triggering a real sense of happiness.

Leo's anecdote refers to a totally different experience of school learning. When asked about a great experience at secondary school, he cannot think of anything, even after being repeatedly encouraged. He 'ponders' (*grübelt*), which in German is a word for a strenuous search in memory that comes to nothing, visible in his facial expression as helplessness, disappointment and even despair. For the life of him, nothing comes to mind that could answer the question satisfactorily.

Not one good school experience in four years of secondary school? Can that be? How is that possible? It must be frustrating to look back and search one's memory for one good experience without finding anything. The researcher helps Leo out of his ruminations by linking the question to a profession that should interest him. Leo stops brooding. He now answers 'firmly', in the German version *bestimmt*, which means clearly and distinctly, no longer unsettled as when he was brooding. Now, Leo knows the best thing about his school experience: that school was over, and he was able to complete his compulsory education at a school with future career prospects, the Polytechnic. Looking back on school, it was void of pleasant memories for him, but the transition from this school to a school with a vocational orientation made his eyes light up.

These anecdotes are just two from a rich pool in which school experiences of learning are expressed in all their diversity, ranging from delightful to disappointing. The project focused on the lower secondary level, which follows primary school and can either be followed by the upper secondary level or lead to vocational training. The importance of anecdote research in the school sector lies in the fact that pupils' recollected experiences offer data for reflection on the organization of school learning. Brigitta's case shows how gratifying participative moments in everyday school life can be and how important it was for her to be allowed to work on something independently for once. This opportunity only opened up for Leo when he left school with the prospect of practical training. Between these two poles lies a wealth of different experiences and memories that provide insights into how learners remember school.

Consequently, anecdotes can lead to important insights about the school as an institution, learning arrangements and didactic issues, and even the importance of teachers' attitudes, as shown in the following anecdote from a focus group of female students. Pupils are susceptible to how teachers engage with them. They are compassionate when it comes to fairness in dealing with praise, as the case of Ms Krismer shows.

Anecdote 15

Peter, Anna and Kerim grumble about Ms Krismer, their teacher. They remember a situation when a university student was teaching in the classroom. 'I didn't hear it quite right', says Kerim, 'but Ms Krismer said to the student, 'Praise Sherad and Andre', and then he came to the front and praised them both. 'But at the beginning, before she said that', adds Anna, 'he said to everyone that they had worked well.' The others confirm this. 'And then she said, yes, he should praise them in particular', Kerim says indignantly, 'like that, we did not do as well as them.' When asked whether they felt this was unfair, they all nodded. 'Yes, the whole school is unfair. I absolutely hate it all the time', Kerim bursts out. (Ammann et al. 2017: 195)

The value students perceive in learning at school does not always align with the lesson plan. In the following anecdote, Yasi draws a surprising conclusion about what he could use from school later in his career:

Anecdote 16

Yasi would like to do an apprenticeship as a carpenter. What can he use from school? Exercise and sport because 'as an apprentice, you often have to run back and forth and chase after things quickly'. Without training, 'you break down' because you are not used to it. So 'you always keep up', he is sure. (Ibid.: 188)

This astonishing assessment could be depressing if Yasi had really learned nothing else for his later life. Yasi, in particular, shows that anecdote research does not narrow down meanings but rather unfolds them, thereby enabling differentiated insights that indeed do justice to the diversity of learning at school. As he says in another anecdote,

> 'School gives you an idea of different things, and you don't go into life having never heard of that; you have never heard of English or maths functions and that', explains Yasi. 'So you learn', he summarizes the purpose of school in three words. 'How can I use it for the future? Yes, for example, that I've heard of everything before, that it's not completely new to me', he explains thoughtfully. (Ibid.)

7.2 Anecdotes as an approach to research on privilege and disadvantage in education

A crucial question for education are the structural, personal and social conditions for disadvantage and privilege. The analyses of Pierre Bourdieu and Jean Claude Passeron (1990) about the strong influence of family and socio-economic background and the resulting differences in the distribution of cultural capital on educational opportunities have sensitized educational science. There are multiple empirical findings that young people from so-called *non-academic* families, in which no family member has received higher education, are significantly less likely to choose to study at university (Peterlini et al. 2022; cf. Jaeger and Karlson 2018). Conversely, the cultural capital enriched in families with positive experiences in university education careers is an encouragement and facilitator for university studies. The resulting questions were addressed at the University of Klagenfurt with a project about motivations and barriers for or against university studies (Peterlini et al. 2023).[2] To this end, a mixed methods design combined a quantitative survey of students with anecdote research. While the quantitative survey provides an impressive overview of motivations for or against studying at university, the anecdotes provide more differentiated insights. The experiences recalled in the anecdotes and their influence on future decisions were exciting.

Anecdote 17

> Alexandra's parents both went to university and told her a lot about that time. Nodding, she says that she has the confidence to go to university. 'Because I also learned from my parents', she thinks for a moment, looks up and says happily, 'from an early age that university is actually the best time'. Alexandra smiles and looks up dreamily. 'Where you can learn so much and when you-' The young woman pauses briefly and continues: 'Where you can also learn what you want'. She thinks about it and adds, babbling: 'at best'. Alexandra laughs and explains her ideas. 'Where you get to meet lots of new people, where you can have lots of first experiences in the', she makes quotation marks in the air with her fingers and says with a grin, '"adult world", so to speak, but where you can still get away with a lot'. She looks up, thinks for a moment and adds in a firm voice: 'It was clear from the beginning that I-' Alexandra interrupts herself and then says quickly with a firm look: 'Well, I never imagined anything other than studying.' She finishes her statement nodding. (Project 18406, Anecdote w5: 1, unpublished)

At first glance, the anecdote is an almost simple confirmation of the theory of educational inheritance: Alexandra was told by her parents, who both went to university, how wonderful it was to study and what opportunities it offered. She, therefore, has positive role models and, as can be surmised from the context, also the necessary prerequisites in terms of cultural, economic and social capital, which, according to Bourdieu (1986), are of great importance for successful educational pathways. However, the descriptive parts of the anecdote stimulate a more differentiated reading. When recalling her parents' stories, she nods to herself, pauses, ponders, then suddenly speaks faster, looks up, ponders again and then speaks in a firm voice. It seems as if everything is clear from her parents' point of view, but she still needs to find her own connection to this family narrative. While she knows from her parents how cool studying at university is, she seems to need her own personal approach to this world so that it genuinely becomes her decision and not a mere repetition of her parents' experiences. Even in the last sentence, in which she declares that it was always clear to her that she would study at university, she interrupts herself, only to finish 'with a steady gaze' and then nod again. What seems clear on the verbal level betrays a struggle on the physical level to ensure that her parents' attitude towards her studies does not overshadow her decision-making, that amidst all this privileged opportunity to study, she still finds the leeway to ensure that this is truly her own decision and not merely the fulfilment of a parental agenda. In this way, the anecdote shows the potential to perceive supposedly unambiguous situations and simple causal relationships more refinedly to make ambivalences visible. Yes, studying is easier if you come from a privileged home, but it involves the burden of emancipating yourself from a privileged status. This multifaceted perspective is even more vividly reflected in the following anecdote from Alexandra about her choice of degree program.

Anecdote 18

Alexandra tells us that she would like to study singing in Vienna. 'Why singing?' Alexandra asks herself, smiling. She straightens up and says: 'I have been singing now since–' Alexandra interrupts herself and says in a firm voice, nodding: 'I mean, classical singing'. Smiling, she tells us she has been playing the violin for ten years. 'Somehow I got into singing', Alexandra pauses briefly and makes a preemptive hand gesture before continuing quickly, 'through a friend'. She looks straight ahead and says, beaming: 'It fascinated me.' Alexandra smiles and says she has 'a lot of contact with music', partly because she attends the music branch at school. She then looks up, thinks about it and says: 'I really began to love music totally' and emphasizes that 'it has become stronger and stronger'. Alexandra explains she has 'progressed quite quickly, quite far' and that this has 'naturally motivated her'. She smiles and says that she then realizes that it is something she could also do professionally later on. Alexandra wants to continue, stops for a moment and makes a hand gesture upwards: 'It could not be better if you can do what you love as a career', she says, beaming and slightly embarrassed at the same time. 'I want', Alexandra pauses momentarily, nods and continues excitedly, 'to go into the opera.' Alexandra exhales loudly, laughs and continues, nodding: 'So that's the plan.' She beams and confirms her statement with a loud 'yes'. (Project 18406, Anecdote w5: 2, unpublished)

At first glance, this could be again an anecdote of privilege. Violin lessons are a characteristic of higher socio-economic classes. What is interesting is that Alexandra hesitates when she presents her decision – not for the violin but for singing. Moreover, she did not come to this decision through her parents but through a friend. Alexandra talks about the violin with a smile, as if it should not be taken too seriously. When it comes to singing however, she talks about her absolute love of music and her own achievements that have motivated her. She holds back her desire to go to the opera for a moment. On the one hand, this is the stage of elitist high culture par excellence, but on the other, it means defending such a wish to her peers, many of whom probably shake their heads. Once again, Alexandra's anecdotes show that the inheritance of education can indeed create initial start challenges and empowerment but does not necessarily spare one from their own emancipatory efforts.

Another interesting finding from the research project was that the focus on family conditions is sometimes too reductive. Peer groups also have a remarkable influence, both supporting and inhibiting. In one anecdote, Amina recounts how she would have liked to study but then fell into the 'wrong circle of friends' and neglected school. A sad moment in the vignette is her question to herself: 'What good are friends like that if you end up with no degree, no nothing?' In the conversation on the base of the anecdote, she mentions her dream job as a hairdresser but comes back to talk about her studies:

Anecdote 19

Amina names 'hairdresser' as her dream job. No, she says firmly, she currently has no interest in pursuing a degree, 'that would not be for me'. In an unemotional tone, she adds that she would 'actually consider' studying. Amina briefly considers and adds with a sheepish laugh: 'If I could overcome my laziness, I would have done it already.' Nodding confidently, she repeats her self-assessment: 'I would be capable of it', and explains seriously: 'If I set a goal for myself, I want to achieve it.' Amina presses her lips together. (Project 18406, Anecdote w1: 9, unpublished)

The anecdote provides a variety of insights into the topic of the research project. One crucial aspect is the question of guilt: in the first anecdote, only paraphrased here, Amina blames the wrong circle of friends in a bitter tone of voice; in the second, she blames herself by referring to her 'laziness'. She does not mention other reasons, such as her origins or poor socio-economic starting conditions. Such assigning of blame to friends and herself reveals the problem of the currently dominant educational discourse of an autonomously conceived subject who, on the one hand, is thought to be endowed with the superpower of self-education and empowerment but who, on the other hand, is also held responsible for the lack of success (see Peterlini 2024). The co-responsibility of social conditions and exclusionary educational institutions, which are blind to educational disadvantage and thus reinforce it, does not even occur to Amina. Instead, the failure is internalized or extended to the wrong circle of friends. For example, she considers pursuing a higher education to be 'not for me', even though, as she encourages herself, she would be capable of it. Her pursed lips express a contradiction for which she cannot find the words – in the face of elitist educational discourses that blame her.

Particularly in selective school systems, young people from educationally disadvantaged backgrounds are often not encouraged to pursue more ambitious and elitist educational paths. According to Bourdieu's concept of *habitus*, teachers classify them as not gifted and weak due to their insecurity in the unfamiliar canon of an educated understanding of knowledge. Consequently, they often cannot free themselves from these prejudices throughout their entire school career, instead internalizing them as supposed objective facts. Pupils from educationally disadvantaged backgrounds are called to the blackboard less often. If they are, they appear insecure, hold back in group work and do not dare to present themselves confidently. Finally, they adapt their self-confidence to the mostly average to low grades they receive. Sentences such as 'I would not advise you to pursue a degree' often linger for many years and ultimately lead to those affected not even considering the decision to pursue higher education, even though they might – like Amina – 'actually' consider themselves capable. The importance of a habitus-reflexive awareness among teachers, who perceive and emphasize the strengths of supposedly 'weak' students, is highlighted in the following anecdote:

Anecdote 20

When asked about a positive experience with school that she remembers to this day, Olivia begins her story without hesitation:

'Oh yes', Olivia recalls. She throws her head back and laughs, 'That was at secondary school', she explains, 'I was rather bad at secondary school at first. She emphasizes 'rather bad' and opens her eyes wide. 'Well, just like that ... in the middle range now, not outstandingly bad or outstandingly good, but simply in the middle range', Olivia continues, shrugging her shoulders. 'Then at some point, it just clicked.' Oliva snaps the fingers of her right hand. She smiles with raised eyebrows and small, intense head movements: 'And I started getting good grades. I was much more active and tried harder.' Olivia's voice becomes melodic, her facial expressions varied. 'And then suddenly there was this parent-teacher conference, and I mean, the teacher praised me in all, in all directions', she says with a smile and raised eyebrows, while she continues with vigorous hand movements 'and said, "Wow, she's developed so well, and I know that this girl is going places."' Olivia emphasizes the last two words and then continues quoting her teacher, still with excited hand movements and active facial expressions: '"and she really needs to keep going to school, and I just see a, a bright future ahead for her"', Olivia continues, her eyes shining. 'And I didn't know what to do with myself because it was really nice to hear', Olivia concludes her story and tilts her head. (Project 18406, Anecdote w3: 1, published in Peterlini et al. 2023: 31)

7.3 Anecdotes as an approach to ethnographic research in humanities and social science

As a method that attempts to perceive the spoken with the unspoken and only bodily expressed, anecdote research is fundamentally suitable for all cultural and social science disciplines. In addition to narrative interviews and conversations, as described in the methodological chapter, impromptu storytelling has additional potential in this context. Conversations with passers-by in a city centre, with fellow passengers on a train or with people in precarious situations often reveal deep insights into biographical, lifeworld, socio-economic, cultural, media and political conditions of human existence and their subjective interpretations.

Anecdote 21

On a train travelling from Klagenfurt to Lienz in Austria, where it then continues across the border to Italy into predominantly German-speaking South Tyrol, an older woman and an older man sit opposite each other in a compartment. Both are estimated to be between seventy and seventy-five years old. When the researcher asks if the seat next to the man is free, they both answer in a friendly manner – 'Yes, of course', says the woman and takes her bag from the seat next to her onto her lap, even though the researcher sits down in the free seat next to the man. The woman, presumably from South Tyrol judging by her dialect, looks at the two men in front of her with an alert gaze, clears her throat, looks out of the window, and then back at the men. The train stops, and a woman with two children gets on and walks through the compartment. The older woman smiles briefly, then sighs: 'Yes, it seems to be better here in Austria with the children; in our region the young brats do not want kids anymore.' When the researcher asks her whether this is truly the case, she tells about a young acquaintance who told her that, no, having a child was out of the question, she would rather have a dog. 'Then I said to her, aha, then I guess the dog will pay your pension – she was quiet, she didn't say anything else.' The older woman interlaces her fingers, sighs again and says that it is also difficult with children; in her village, the locals are getting evicted because they can no longer pay the rent. 'And then they put the migrants in because the state pays for them and the money arrives on time – that's how it is in South Tyrol.' The man from East Tyrol interrupts her, 'Well, it is not just like that in South Tyrol, it's the same here, the migrants get everything.' 'Really', marvels the woman from South Tyrol, 'my God, soon we will have more foreigners than our people here, well, well'. When the researcher asks again whether that can be true, she frowns: 'You can believe me, that's how it is, and if you get sick, nobody will help you anymore, the doctors will just look at the computer instead of examining you.' (Interview transcript by the author from 15 December 2016)

The anecdote based on a train conversation comes from an ongoing research programme at the University of Klagenfurt on everyday discourses on migration. The statements in the episode reflect stereotypical views that do not correspond to the facts but nevertheless persist in many people's minds. What does the anecdote describe? The woman looks at the men openly. She is probably looking for a conversation; this points to a generation that does not sit silently next to each other in trains or subways and look fixedly in front of them or at the smartphone but instead likes to engage in dialogue. The woman who boards the train with her two children and walks through the compartment gives the old woman a cue. She mentions the declining birth rates in Italy, which do not apply to the same extent to the predominantly German-speaking and rather conservative South Tyrol. However, South Tyrol, once part of the Austro-Hungarian Empire, was annexed by Italy in the Second World War. The woman's perception also incorporates a subtle political distinction. She contrasts the decline in birth rates in Italy (including South Tyrol) with the supposedly more fertile situation in the former fatherland of Austria – in short, the presumable degenerate situation in Italy with the supposedly ideal world in Austria.

When the Austrian train passenger points out that things are no better there either, the dichotomy between an ideal world and a world that has become problematic shifts to the question of natives and migrants. This short scene shows the power of dichotomies (Peterlini 2019; 2020b) in generating discourses and enemy images from which one's world must be protected. Ultimately, however, it is not the initially blamed young woman who is responsible for the decline in the birth rate, and the woman definitely does not address socio-economic developments. No, in the end, it is the – factually unfounded – discrimination of natives in favour of foreigners that is to blame. When asked by the researcher whether this is true, she initially reacts with irritation, as evident in the wrinkling of her forehead. Then suddenly, the topic of healthcare is brought up, an issue that concerns not only, but particularly, older people in an existential way. The anecdote could serve as an example of how the need to talk about one's concerns first finds a gratifying structure via dichotomous patterns between good and evil: between the bad Italian and the good Austrian conditions, between the women with many children in the past and the young things today, between locals and foreigners. Typically, the latter theme is so powerful that it can remain so – all problems would be gone if only migrants would not come. In this case, however, the researcher meets this narrative with doubt, which initially silences the woman until an authentic, real-life concern comes to light – health, ageing and a healthcare system that no longer takes the time for such concerns for efficiency reasons. The psychoanalytical explanation that thinking in terms of enemy images suppresses existential concerns (illness and mortality, social insecurity, fears about the future due to climate crisis and wars) finds a possible exemplification in the short sequence. Of course, this is only one of many other possible readings of this anecdote; it should illustrate how anecdotes can be fruitful for ethnographic and socio-spatially orientated research.

7.4 Anecdotes as an approach to research on biography and identity building

As a method that brings past experiences back to life in memory and thus makes them accessible for reflection, anecdote research is also particularly suitable for researching how biography and self-development, personal development and social positioning interact. Another area is research in the field of memory culture and cultural heritage, where the narrative approach of anecdote research has exciting applications.

One particular example is the research conducted by Jasmin Donlic at the University of Klagenfurt with young Muslims in Austria on the connection between biography, identity formation and social contexts (Donlic and Yildiz 2022; Donlic 2023). In particular, the focus is on past personal or family experiences of flight or migration, the experiences of growing up in a traditionally and predominantly non-Muslim society and partly under anti-Muslim discourses. The research focuses on the everyday religious practices of second-generation Muslims born, raised and socialized in the Alps-Adriatic region in Carinthia in Austria at the border to Slovenia and Italy. These individuals are developing differentiated forms of religiousness and perspectives on religion. Religious practices are often regarded as a mere continuation of Islamic traditions in the countries from which their parent generation migrated. However, this generation practices religion in ways shaped by socialization in a largely secularized postmodern society and by inter-religiosity, that is, interaction between people with different beliefs that provokes them to reflect on attitudes and alter their perspectives. Whereas their parents or grandparents more or less lived in their own bubble, mainly because they did not speak the language well enough, the new generation sees inter-religious interaction and communication as a matter of course – part of the everyday practices they take for granted. The research combines phenomenological anecdote research with a participatory approach. In this way, the young people are involved in the reading and interpretation process of the anecdotes based on their interviews and stimulated by photographs according to the PhotoVoice Method (see Donlic 2023).

Anecdote 22

When asked what role religion plays in her everyday life, Esra looks up and nods. She explains firmly that she thinks about God in her everyday life and that she says her prayers, especially before going to bed. Sitting up straight and with a broad grin, Esra says in a clear and firm voice: 'Normal Muslims who live the faith as it is set down, let's say – that is, not strictly religiously – didn't change this; this is what Islam says, as it was taught 100 years ago, as our grandmothers, grandfathers, and so on lived it: for me, these were normal Muslims.' She continues to grin, loudly emphasising the words 'normal Muslims' and adds energetically, 'I drink alcohol and actually try not to put the word God in my mouth when I've been drinking alcohol.' (Ibid.: 10)

Anecdote 23

Samira recalls coming across a Ramadan calendar containing chocolates while shopping. 'A Ramadan chocolate calendar is a really cool idea', Samira observes excitedly. Speaking in a proud tone, she puffs out her chest. 'We were all delighted to buy some because you only ever really know the Advent calendars you got from your parents.' Samira bought the Ramadan chocolate calendar to 'support the idea, somehow'. She told everyone around her to buy more to strengthen demand in Austria, too, and 'then maybe there will be more choice in the future, and it will become more common'. Media coverage of the idea led parents to start making their own Ramadan calendars for their children. Samira tells the story with a smile and leans back: 'Then I thought, okay, so it would be a nice idea.' Samira gave her Austrian neighbours a Ramadan calendar 'because they're sort of happy for us, even though the holiday doesn't mean anything to them'. For Samira, this is a happy event. She is beaming. (Ibid.: 7)

These are only two of a wide range of anecdotes collected by interviews with young female and male Muslims in Carinthia. The researcher (Donlic 2023) analyses them in this way:

In public discourse in particular, with hybrid behaviours such as drinking alcohol (as seen in Esra's example), young people are beginning to make small adjustments to their religioness (Yildiz 2020: 23), and these religious orientations and reorientations are accompanied by inter-religious understanding. Someone who drinks alcohol, but adopts the ritual of not drinking before Eid and the Feast of Sacrifice, is demonstrating religious flexibility. New Muslim generations are beginning to set their own rules and negotiate their own access to their religion. ... The headscarf is generally discussed in public discourse as being perceived 'negatively'. Wearing the headscarf in the professional world and in everyday life often provokes discrimination and racism, as Esmira's example shows. Young women are starting to resist and discuss cultural stereotypes and to develop their own strategies. Esmira's experience shows that the way she wears and ties the headscarf can also create a stir. As bell hooks (1989) explained, speaking about such experiences can be seen as an empowering act. Samira's Advent calendar, meanwhile, indicates that new Muslim generations have a transcultural understanding of time. This appropriation and transcoding (Hall 1994) into a Ramadan calendar can be understood as inter-religious education (Yıldız 2020: 24), emerging as historical normality, uncovering other experiences and forms of knowledge, telling other stories. (Donlic 2023: 11)

7.5 Anecdotes as a reflection tool for professional and organizational development and evaluation in different contexts

In discussing anecdotes as a scholarly tool (Chapter 1), we have already pointed out how even medical and other propositional sciences – despite their scepticism about the validity of anecdotal knowledge – consider anecdotes suitable for training and evaluation processes (Macnaughton 1995: 571). Here is an example of an impromptu conversation with a patient in an Austrian hospital:

Anecdote 24

'Yes, that was then …' Peter hesitates briefly, takes a breath, then continues: '… uh after my hip operation. I was lying there on the hospital bed, I think it was pretty much right after the operation or when I woke up …' Again, Peter falters and straightens up a bit. 'I was still in a lot of pain, yeah, phew, it hurt like hell. And at the same time, I was so happy when the doctors told me everything had gone well. I was so happy …' Peter falls silent and smiles sheepishly, shrugging his shoulders; he backs away a little further, 'Yes, I had tears, I, who am otherwise like a bear … my wife always says.' Peter laughs, then suddenly narrows his eyes. 'There is only one thing I still don't understand, and that's that I'm lying there, I'm in a lot of pain, and then the doctor barks at the nurse I think it was the first examination, 'who did this crap?' And she pulls on the tubes and gets nervous, 'Give me the scissors!' The nurse gets nervous and doesn't find the right scissors, then the doctor rummages around somewhere in the instrument case, takes something out, pulls again, snips and continues to argue with the nurse, who makes a grim face but says nothing more.' Peter seems distraught by the story; he looks up and says: 'Can you imagine, you are lying there, they are arguing and tearing at you, and you can't say anything. I thought, do they even notice that I'm there too?' (Anecdote, 4 June 2023, unpublished)

EXAMPLES OF APPLICATIONS 135

Such an anecdote can provide illuminating points of reference for reflecting on communication and cooperation in the presence of patients. Such applications are still uncharted territory for anecdote research. However, the initial trials are promising and open up a wide range of possible applications, including participatory self-evaluations by different organizations.

Below are two anecdotes by Alina Revelant (2023) from her study on power relations in social organizations.

Anecdote 25

With slumped shoulders, Anja says, 'in the organization where I worked, I didn't have the feeling that I was being listened to in any way'. She emphasizes, 'You didn't have a say.' Gradually, she realized that the power from the top was decisive for the negative development of the employees' well-being. 'You were somehow a bit ... sometimes I felt like an idiot ... left standing because you expressed your opinion, criticism, or worries.' Anja looks at the cat and thoughtfully repeats what she has been told by the team leader in such situations: 'Shut up, how do you think I feel? This has no place now.' Looking down, she sips her tea. (Ibid.)

Anecdote 26

When Anja comes to talk about the atmosphere in the team, she thinks for a moment and takes a big sip of tea. 'You could tell who was a thorn in someone's side, ... then they acted accordingly.' She recounts with dismay that colleagues were 'interrupted, cut off, ignored, ignored' and that this made her 'feel out of place and uncomfortable'. She had realized 'that the employees were simply cannon powder that had been fired', although they were actually the 'foundation'. Lost in thought, she begins to stroke her cat and suddenly bursts out that the inpatient area of child and youth welfare is a 'miniverse', 'a small dictatorship' in which one has to function. (Ibid.)

The anecdotes speak for themselves and will not be interpreted further here. What is interesting, however, is the role that the cat, which would hardly be relevant in a conventional interview, is given by the descriptive elements of the anecdote. In the first anecdote, it is the look at the cat that helps Anja to describe the attitude of the team leader once again clearly. She then falls silent and sips her tea. In the second anecdote, stroking the cat as if it were her power animal suddenly brings out her dissatisfaction, her resentment that her work environment is run like a dictatorship in which one is expected to simply function.

How do we deal with such anecdotes? Confronting the management and staff of an organization with the anecdotes that have emerged during its evaluation can be problematic (see Section 6.3). A more manageable and no less effectual approach to reflect on anecdotes from another similar organization during training courses and reflection workshops, as this can inevitably make power dynamics in one's organization a topic of discussion. In the narrower sense of an evaluation project, the evaluation team will look carefully at how it can utilize the knowledge gained from the anecdotes in suitable settings and at the appropriate levels. In some instances, anecdotes can also be discussed in individual departments concerned or with different levels of management but without exposing the people involved in the anecdote to direct embarrassment or the risk of discrimination. The anonymity of the persons speaking in the anecdote and those otherwise involved must always be preserved!

A productive value of the anecdote for the organization it concerns lies in its creation and validation. Allowing employees to talk about their state of mind, workflow and organizational structures in interviews or impromptu conversations can trigger reflection processes. If possible, it is advisable to reflect on the anecdote afterwards with the person or people who primarily contributed to it through their narrative. This setting allows them to reflect once again on the problem revealed in the anecdote. It can stimulate new awareness processes, which can be interesting for evaluation and personnel development. The resulting questions can be the following: what options for action does the employee who feels so oppressed have? Do others feel the same way? Can similar experiences be shared in order to strengthen staff in this way? Can the employees perhaps collaboratively develop a strategy to demand a more friendly approach from management?

7.6 Anecdotes as a tool for professional development in different contexts

The anecdotes presented here are just a few examples of applications in different disciplines and settings. Furthermore, as mentioned in the example of the medical professions, anecdotes are also suitable for training and further education in academic and professional settings.

The following is an anecdote from a day-care centre where children aged six months to three years are looked after.

Anecdote 27

> As she talks about her work with one-year-old Simona, Petra grabs her ears with both hands and covers them for a moment: 'You have no idea how she screams', she says in a loud tone, 'nobody can stand that for long, I'll go to the toilet so I can calm down'. Petra has also spoken to the manager about Simona, 'but the boss is covered in red tape, yes, she said she would speak to the parents in two months'. Simona was actually quite 'normal' when she first came to the daycare centre, but then suddenly nothing worked anymore: 'As soon as you don't pay attention to her, she screams. The best way to deal with this is to leave her in the pram. She just sits there all day, we even feed her while she's in the pram', shrugs Petra. 'But if you move away for even a moment, she screams.' She spoke to the parents once, but they said that she was completely normal at home and that Simona was probably just fooling the staff. 'This child is impossible, I hope the psychologist comes soon, because ...' She bangs heavily on the table and almost shouts: 'Because she's definitely got something, she's got something. She's definitely got something.' When Petra sees the stunned look on my face, she pauses and says, 'Sorry, sometimes it all gets too much for me.' (Anecdote, 22 May 2023, unpublished)

The anecdote comes from a university student who interviewed Petra, her friend. It expresses complex problems that allow for reflection, for instance, on leadership, pedagogical attitude, the reliance on diagnoses, the pressure of the institutions between authorities and parents and much more. One of the questions raised in the seminar was what training Petra has had that makes her talk about the children in such an unprofessional manner. The seminar group in resonance reading also discusses solution strategies: a parent–teacher conference earlier than planned, more decisive involvement of the manager or simply considering wrapping Simona in a baby sling instead of letting her cry. The students cannot directly influence Petra and Simona and change their situation. What they learn is how to deal with difficult situations and discuss them from different perspectives, which can benefit their practice later on. Similarly, medical or technology students could be trained in short training modules to hold conversations with patients, paramedics, construction workers or users of technical equipment and to create anecdotes based on these interactions. Alternatively, discussions could be held with them using anecdotes from their fields of training or work to identify issues related to patient perceptions in hospitals or experiences of technical staff or customers and to discuss better approaches to handling these situations.

In summary, it can be said that the anecdote serves as a research and evaluation instrument suitable for a wide range of academic and practical applications, as its use can be tailored to meet specific professional and organizational needs. The anecdote gets stimulating content from conversations in which people recall and reveal their experiences, thus making these experiences present and accessible for reflection. The unique combination of verbal and bodily speech also calls suppressed and repressed elements into awareness. The multidimensional and versatile nature of reading and interpreting anecdotes prevents rigid objectification and facilitates an exchange of perspectives and viewpoints that can be productive for scholars while at the same time opening up exploration and expanding options for action.

Notes

1 'Poly' means the Polytechnic School, which in Austria covers the ninth compulsory school year if no upper secondary school is attended.
2 'Be First! Aber wie? Perspektiven auf Beweggründe und Barrieren für oder gegen die Aufnahme eines Hochschulstudiums', Project 18406 funded by Jubilee Fund of the Austrian National Bank, 2020-2, project leader Hans Karl Peterlini, University of Klagenfurt.

CHAPTER 8

Looking back and ahead

Looking back on the book having now reached the end, we hope we have offered you a coherent and stimulating presentation of the genesis, development and application of anecdote research. As readers, you should now have in your hands an instrument for research at a crucial intersection for the academic understanding of humans in the dimensions of time, space and body. Anecdotes recount the recalled experiences of individual people; they provide insights into individual biographies and memorable moments of fulfilment or rupture of those moments that are important to people in retrospect. Otherwise, they would not recount them.

Following the phenomenological assumption that individual examples reveal general phenomena of life and the world, they also have an intersubjective cognitive value. Even at the very moment an anecdote emerges – during an interview, a conversation or an impromptu story – the narrative at its core is not only individual. It owes its existence to varied and complex interactions and social relationships in the past; it arises in a conversation between people in a space that cannot be closed off due to scholarly interest in knowledge but must remain open to the outside world, preserving course anonymity and personal rights.

The anecdote is, therefore, individual and interpersonal; it is historical, present and also directed towards the future; it is verbal, bodily and inter-bodily. It arises and operates in a multifaceted in-between: between past, present and future, between the narrator and the listener and between body and world. This multifaceted nature is the reason for the intersubjective, supratemporal and inter-bodily character of the anecdote. Its expressive value comes from the personal and transcends it; it is biographical and opens up the biography to change; it is the expression of a bodily person in his or her lifeworld and becoming a subject.

The empirical craft of working with anecdotes may seem manageable and even too simple, given the widespread tendency to secure evidence through ever more sophisticated and complex mechanized and digitalized procedures. What does anecdote research require? The first step is to listen, look and empathize. That sounds simple, but it involves a constantly balanced attitude between distance and attentiveness, allowing the other person to be with themselves and open up. In the second step, in which the conversation becomes an anecdote, a different balance is essential: academic rigour and creative design.

Writing anecdotes takes the courage to reassemble parts of interviews or conversations, to condense them into a story, to let them lead to a punch line – this is literary work with a scholarly claim. At the same time, writing anecdotes requires the utmost care to preserve what has been said, not to interpret or even bend the possible meaning according to the researcher's interests, to explore blind spots in dealing with the data material as best possible, in order to create a concise text, in which the phenomenological surplus of what has been experienced and remembered is saved for the search for knowledge.

Such a method of dealing with human narratives is no better than other methods that, for example, search and code the interviews according to predetermined categories or developed from the material, record them digitally, filter them according to fixed sequences or analyse them as 'neutrally' as possible using software. Anecdote research promises no more insight than other empirical approaches to human storytelling. This method will miss some things that other approaches bring to light. It brings to light insights that other methods miss. Every method brings aspects of reality to light and inevitably leaves others in the shadows. Anecdote research makes it possible for people to recall their experiences and condense them through the art form of the anecdote to give them lasting value for ever-new understandings of human learning and becoming, suffering and action. What is verbalized in an anecdote today can open up different perspectives for understanding people and the world tomorrow, the morning after and in 100 years.

The meaning of an anecdote is just as little exhausted with its writing as with its first interpretations; every time one reads it, the meaning of the anecdote is created anew – between the text and the reader, between the remembered episode, the time of writing and the moment of reading. The academic validity is guaranteed by maintaining the phenomenological attitude: not searching for an essence of truth but asking what is revealed in the anecdote from the respective perspective of the reader. This process is never concluded; the possible insights are always new and never final, and they leave space for other insights from other perspectives. Phenomenology is an adventure in a firm empirical stance with an open outcome.

In the history of phenomenology, anecdote research is still a young method that needs further testing. Nevertheless, the examples presented should have shown the potential of anecdotes. As firmly as the academic creation of anecdotes is anchored in phenomenology, the anecdotes are open to interpretation and application from the perspective of other disciplinary approaches and demands. That is an essential feature of the phenomenological research approach: the perception of phenomena requires a rigorous scientific attitude, but their interpretation and the use of findings are open to different and interdisciplinary research interests and applications.

In this sense, anecdotes, as a linguistic condensation of remembered experience, are crystallization points for a deeper and broader understanding of learning processes in the broadest sense, with breaks and further developments. In an individual confrontation, in dialogue and multi-perspective exchange with others, in scholarly interpretation and practice-oriented application, impulses and suggestions, inspirations and provocations arise for the ever-new understanding of man and the world in their unfathomable but not wholly closed to human understanding interaction.

We do not see the book as a complete treatise but as an impetus to continue working with anecdotes. We hope we have encouraged you to do so.

REFERENCES

Adams, H. F. (1936). 'Validity, Reliability, and Objectivity'. *Psychological Monographs*, 47 (2), 329–50. Available online: https://doi.org/10.1037/h0093421 (accessed 5 January 2024).

Agostini, E. (2016a). *Lernen im Spannungsfeld von Finden und Erfinden. Zur schöpferischen Genese von Sinn im Vollzug der Erfahrung.* Paderborn: Schöningh.

Agostini, E. (2016b). 'Lektüre von Vignetten. Reflexive Zugriffe auf Erfahrungsvollzüge des Lernens'. In S. Baur and H. K. Peterlini (eds), *An der Seite des Lernens. Erfahrungsorientierte Bildungsforschung*, vol 2. Vienna: StudienVerlag, 55–62.

Agostini, E. (2020). 'Lernen "am Fall" versus Lernen "am Beispiel". Oder: Zur Bedeutung der pathischen Struktur ästhetischer Wahrnehmung für die Narration von phänomenologisch orientierten Vignetten'. In H. K. Peterlini, I. Cennamo and J. Donlic (eds), *Wahrnehmung als pädagogische Übung. Theoretische und praxisorientierte Auslotungen einer phänomenologisch orientierten Bildungsforschung*. Erfahrungsorientierte Bildungsforschung, vol. 7. Innsbruck: StudienVerlag, 153–78.

Agostini, E., and H. K. Peterlini (2022). 'Vignette Research. An Austrian Phenomenological Approach to Empirical Research'. In T. Fedges (ed.), *Education in Europe: Contemporary Approaches across the Continent*. London: Routledge, 130–40. Available online: https://www.taylorfrancis.com/chapters/edit/10.4324/9781003223528-14/vignette-research-evi-agostini-hans-karl-peterlini (accessed 4 January 2024).

Agostini, E., H. K. Peterlini and M. Schratz (2019). 'Pädagogik der Leiblichkeit? Phänomenologische und praxistheoretische Perspektiven auf leibliche Erfahrungsvollzüge in Schule und Unterricht'. In M. Brinkmann, J. Türstig and M. Weber-Spanknebel (eds), *Leib – Leiblichkeit – Embodiment. Pädagogische Perspektiven auf eine Phänomenologie des Leibes*. Phänomenologische Erziehungswissenschaft, vol. 8. Wiesbaden: Springer VS.

Agostini, E., H. K. Peterlini, J. Donlic, V. Kumpusch, D. Lehner and I. Sandner (eds) (2023). *The Vignette as an Exercise in Perception. On the Professionalization of Educational Practices*. Opladen: Barbara

Budrich. Available online: https://doi.org/10.3224/84742662 (accessed 30 November 2023).

Agostini, E., I. Eloff and M. Schratz (2024). *Vignette Research. Research Methods*. London: Bloomsbury Academic.

Albertazzi, L. (1999). *Shapes of Forms. From Gestalt Psychology and Phenomenology to Ontology and Mathematics*. Dordrecht: Springer. Available online: https://doi.org/10.1007/978-94-017-2990-1 (accessed 10 December 2023).

Alvesson, M., and J. Sandberg (2022). 'Pre-Understanding: An Interpretation-Enhancer and Horizon-Expander in Research'. *Organization Studies*, 43 (3), 395–412. Available online: https://doi.org/10.1177/0170840621994507 (accessed 8 August 2023).

Ammann, M. (2017a). 'Lektüre von Vignetten und Anekdoten – Markierungsversuche'. In M. Ammann, T. Westfall-Greiter and M. Schratz (eds), *Erfahrungen deuten – Deutungen erfahren. Experiential Vignettes and Anecdotes as Research, Evaluation and Mentoring Tool*. Erfahrungsorientierte Bildungsforschung, vol. 3. Innsbruck: StudienVerlag, 153–61.

Ammann, M. (2017b). 'Vertrauen in der Schule – ein facettenreiches Phänomen'. In M. Ammann, T. Westfall-Greiter and M. Schratz (eds), *Erfahrungen deuten – Deutungen erfahren. Experiential Vignettes and Anecdotes as Research, Evaluation and Mentoring Tool*. Erfahrungsorientierte Bildungsforschung, vol. 3. Innsbruck: StudienVerlag, 183–6.

Ammann, M., S. Krenn, G. Rathgeb, A. Winder and M. Schratz (2017). 'Anekdoten – eine Auswahl'. In M. Ammann, T. Westfall-Greiter and M. Schratz (eds), *Erfahrungen deuten – Deutungen erfahren. Experiential Vignettes and Anecdotes as Research, Evaluation and Mentoring Tool*. Erfahrungsorientierte Bildungsforschung, vol. 3. Innsbruck: StudienVerlag, 187–96.

Ammann, M., T. Westfall-Greiter and M. Schratz (eds) (2017). *Erfahrungen deuten – Deutungen erfahren. Experiential Vignettes and Anecdotes as Research, Evaluation and Mentoring Tool*. Erfahrungsorientierte Bildungsforschung, vol. 3. Innsbruck: StudienVerlag.

Arbeitsgruppe Bielefelder Soziologen (1976). *Kommunikative Sozialforschung. Alltagswissen und Alltagshandeln – Gemeindemachtforschung – Polizei – Politische Entwicklung*. München: Wilhelm.

Arendt, H. (1958). *The Human Condition*. Chicago: University of Chicago Press.

Arendt, H. ([1963] 2006). *Eichmann in Jerusalem. A Report on the Banality of Evil*. London: Penguin.

Arrighetti, G. (2007). 'Anekdote und Biographie'. In M. Erler and S. Schorn (eds), *Die griechische Biographie in hellenistischer Zeit. Akten des internationalen Kongresses vom 26.-29. Juli 2006 in Würzburg*. Berlin: De Gruyter, 79–100.
Assmann, A. (2015). 'Dialogic Memory'. In P. Mendes-Flohr (ed.), *Dialogue as a Trans-Disciplinary Concept: Martin Buber's Philosophy of Dialogue and Its Contemporary Reception*. Berlin: De Gruyter, 199–214. https://doi.org/10.1515/9783110402223-013 (accessed 18 January 2024).
Assmann, J. (2002). *Das kulturelle Gedächtnis. Schrift, Erinnerung und politische Identität in frühen Hochkulturen*. 4th edition. Munich: Verlag Ch. Beck.
Assmann, J. (2011). *Cultural Memory and Early Civilization: Writing, Remembrance, and Political Imagination*. Cambridge: Cambridge University Press.
Bachelard, G. (1990). *Fragments of a Poetics of Fire*. Dallas: Dallas Institute Publications.
Beekman, T. (1983). *On 'Participant Experience' with Children. Paper Given at Second Annual Human Science Conference*. Pittsburgh, PA: Duquesne University.
Beekman, T. (1987). 'Hand in Hand mit Sascha. Über Glühwürmchen, Grandma Millie und einige andere Raumgeschichten. Im Anhang: Über teilnehmende Erfahrung'. In W. Lippitz and K. Meyer-Drawe (eds), *Kind und Welt*. Frankfurt a.M.: Athenäum, 11–24.
Bell, B. (1994). 'Using Anecdotes in Teacher Development'. *International Journal of Science Education*, 16, 575–84.
Bengtsson, J. (2002). 'Phenomenological Ethics, a Historical Outline'. In A. T. Tymieniecka (ed.), *Phenomenology World-Wide. Analecta Husserliana*, vol. 80. Dordrecht: Springer, 520–32. Available online: https://doi.org/10.1007/978-94-007-0473-2_56 (accessed 13 September 2023).
Blumenberg, H. (1988). *Der Prozeß der theoretischen Neugierde*. 4th and revised edition. Frankfurt: Suhrkamp.
Boal, A. (1993). *Theatre of the Oppressed*. New York: Theatre Communications Group.
Bourdieu, P. (1986). 'The Forms of Capital'. In J. G. Richardson (ed.), *Handbook of Theory and Research in the Sociology of Education*. New York: Greenwood Press, 241–58.
Bourdieu, P., and J. C. Passeron (1990). *Reproduction in Education, Society and Culture*. London: SAGE.
Bozzi, P. (1999). 'Experimental Phenomenology: A Historical Profile'. In Liliana Albertazzi (ed.), *Shapes of Forms. From Gestalt Psychology*

and Phenomenology to Ontology and Mathematics. Synthese Libraray 275. Dordrecht: Springer, 19–50.

Brinkmann, S, and S. Kvale (2018). 'Doing Interviews'. *Second, Qualitative Research Kit*. 55. London: SAGE. Available online: https://doi.org/10.4135/9781529716665 (accessed 20 December 2023).

Brinkmann, M. (2020). 'Phänomenologie'. In Gabriele Weiß and Jörg Zirfaß (eds), *Handbuch Bildungs- und Erziehungsphilosophie*. Wiesbaden: Springer, 601–13.

Cambridge Online Dictionary (2019). Available online: https://dictionary.cambridge.org/us/dictionary/english/anecddote (accessed 11 July 2023).

Calvino, I. (1985). *Mr Palomar*. Translated by William Weaver. New York: Harcourt.

Cennamo, I., J. Donlic and H. K. Peterlini (2020). 'Die Vignette im Forschungsdesign. Potenziale, Grenzen und Anknüpfungspunkte einer Methodenkombination am Beispiel einer Antragstellung'. In H. K. Peterlini, I. Cennamo and J. Donlic (eds), *Wahrnehmung als pädagogische Übung. Theoretische und praxisorientierte Auslotungen einer phänomenologisch orientierten Bildungsforschung*. Erfahrungsorientierte Bildungsforschung, vol. 7. Innsbruck: StudienVerlag, 179–99.

Costello, P. R. (2012). *Layers in Husserl's Phenomenology: On Meaning and Intersubjectivity*. Toronto: Toronto University Press.

Crowell, S. (2023). '"Grenzprobleme" of Phenomenology: Metaphysics'. In J. Yoshimi, Ph. Walsh and P. Londen (eds), *Horizons of Phenomenology. Essays on the State of the Field and Its Applications*. Contributions to Phenomenology 122. Cham: Springer, 171–98. Available online: https://doi.org/10.1007/978-3-031-26074-2 (accessed 15 December 2023).

Dahlstrom, M. F. (2014). 'Using Narratives and Storytelling to Communicate Science with Nonexpert Audiences'. *PNAS*, 111, supplement 4, 13614–20.

Danner, H. (1995). 'Hermeneutics in Educational Discourse: Foundations'. In P. Higgs (ed.) *Metatheories in Philosophy of Education*. Johannesburg: Heinemann, 221–44.

Danner, H. (2006). *Methoden geisteswisssenschaftlicher Pädagogik*. Munich: Reinhardt UTB.

De Boer, T. (1980). 'Inleiding'. In T. de Boer (ed.), *Edmund Husserl: Filosofie als strenge wetenschap*. Amsterdam: Boom Meppel, 7–32.

Denzin, N. K., and Y. S. Lincoln (2008). *Strategies of Qualitative Inquiry*, vol. 2. London: SAGE.

Dewey, J. ([1934] 1986). 'Art as Experience'. Translated by. H. Schreier. In H. Schreier (ed.), *John Dewey: Erziehung durch und für Erfahrung*. Stuttgart: Ernst Klett-Verlag, S. 220–32.

Donlic J. (2023). 'New Muslim Generations: Shaping Self-Image, Reshaping Religion: A Theoretical and Empirical Study of Inter-Religiosity with Muslim Youth in the Alps-Adriatic Region'. *Religions and Theologies*, 14 (8), 1–15. Available online: https://www.mdpi.com/2077-1444/14/8/993 (accessed 3 January 2024).

Donlic, J., and E. Yildiz (2022). 'Postmuslimische Generation und ihre Lebensentwürfe. Vom Islamdispositiv zu Alltagserfahrungen'. *Forum Islamisch-Theologische Studien*, 1 (1), 85–108.

Faulstich-Wieland, H., and P. Faulstich (2012). *Lebenswege und Lernräume. Martha Muchow: Leben, Werk und Weiterwirken*. Weinheim: Juventa.

Fineman, J. (1989). 'The History of the Anecdote: Fiction and Fiction'. In A. Veeser (ed.), *The New Historicism*. New York: Routledge, 49–76.

Finlay, L. (2009). 'Debating Phenomenological Methods'. *Phenomenology & Practice*, 3 (1), 6–25.

Flick, U. (2018). 'About This Book and Its Second Edition'. In S. Brinkmann and S. Kvale (eds), *Doing Interviews. The Sage Qualitative Research Kit*, 2nd edition. London: SAGE, xv–xvi.

Flick, U., E. von Kardoff and I. Steinke (eds) (2012). *Qualitative Forschung. Ein Handbuch*. 9th edition. Hamburg: Rowohlt Taschenbuch.

Flores D'Arcais, P. (1995). 'Pädagogik – warum und für wen?' In W. Böhm (ed.), *Pädagogik – wozu und für wen?* Stuttgart: Klett-Cotta, 24–42.

Freud, S. ([1900] 1913). *The Interpretation of Dreams*. Translated by Abraham A. Brill. New York: Macmillan Company.

Friesen, N. (2014). 'Waldenfels' Responsive Phenomenology of the Alien: An Introduction'. *Phenomenology & Practice*, 7 (2), 68–77.

Fuchs, T. (2011). 'Erzählen als Bildungserfahrung. Zeitlichkeit und Bildungsbedeutsamkeit lebensgeschichtlicher Erzählungen. Unter Mitarbeit von Mitra Keller'. In O. Hartung, I. Steininger and T. Fuchs (eds), *Lernen und Erzählen interdisziplinär*. Wiesbaden: Springer, 123–45.

Gabriel, G. (2010). 'Kennen und Erkennen'. In J. Bromand and G. Kreis (eds), *Was sich nicht sagen lässt: Das Nicht-Begriffliche in Wissenschaft, Kunst und Religion*. Berlin: Akademic-Verlag, 43–55.

Gadamer, H.-G. (1976). *Philosophie. Hermeneutik. Kleine Schriften*, vol. 1. Tübingen: J. C. B. Mohr.

Gadamer, H.-G. (1986). *Composition and Interpretation. The Relevance of the Beautiful and Other Essays*. Edited by R. Bernasconi, translated by N. Walker. Cambridge: Cambridge University Press.

Gadamer, H.-G. ([1960] 1994). *Truth and Method.* New York: Continuum.
Gehring, P. (2011). 'Ist die Phänomenologie eine Wirklichkeitswissenschaft? Überlegungen zur Aktualität der Phänomenologie und ihrer Verfahren'. In M. Flatscher and I. Laner (eds), *Neue Stimmen der Phänomenologie 1, Die Tradition. Das Selbst.* Nordhausen: Traugott Bautz, 29–47.
Gelhard, A. (2012). *Kritik der Kompetenz.* Zurich: Diophanes.
Giddens, A. (1997). *Die Konstitution der Gesellschaft. Grundzüge einer Theorie der Strukturierung.* Frankfurt a.M.: New York Campus.
Giorgi, A. (1989). 'One Type of Analysis of Descriptive Data: Procedures Involved in Following a Phenomenological Method'. *Methods*, 1, 39–61.
Goethe, J. W. v. ([1810] 1988). *Scientific Studies.* Edited and translated by Miller Douglas. New York: Suhrkamp.
Gossman, L. (2003). 'Anecdote and History'. *History and Theory*, 42 (May), 143–68.
Griffero, T. (2019). 'Introduction. How Do You Find Yourself in Your Environment? Hermann Schmitz's New Phenomenology'. In. H. Schmitz (ed.), *New Phenomenology. A Brief Introduction.* Milan-Udine: Mimesis International, 9–41.
Gutzen, D., N. Oellers and J. H. Petersen (1981). *Einführung in die neuere deutsche Literaturwissenschaft.* 4th edition. Berlin: Schmidt.
Halbwachs, M. (1967). *Das kollektive Gedächtnis.* Stuttgart: Enke.
Hall, St. (1994). 'Das Spektakel des "Anderen"'. In S. Hall (ed.), *Ideologie, Identität, Repräsentation.* Hamburg: Argument, 108–66.
Hamm, R. (2020). '"De-Romanticised and Very ... Different". Models for Distinguishing Practical Applications of Collective Memory-Work'. *Other Education*, 9 (1), 53–90.
Hamm, R. (2021). *Kollektive Erinnerungsarbeit. Anwendungen, Variationen, Adaptionen weltweit.* Hamburg: Argument.
Haraway, D. (2019). 'It Matters What Stories Tell Stories; It Matters Whose Stories Tell Stories'. *A/b: Auto/Biography Studies*, 34 (3), 565–75. Available online: https://doi.org/10.1080/08989575.2019.1664163 (accessed 4 October 2023).
Haug, F. (1999). *Vorlesungen zur Einführung in die Erinnerungsarbeit. The Duke Lectures.* Berlin, Hamburg: Argument.
Hegel, G. W. F. ([1807] 1977). *Phenomenology of Spirit.* Translated by A. V. Miller. Oxford: Oxford University Press.
Hennigfeld, I. (2015). 'Goethe's Phenomenological Way of Thinking and the Urphänomen'. *Goethe Yearbook*, 22, 143–67. Available online: https://doi.org/10.1353/gyr.2015.0036 (accessed 7 October 2023).

Henriksson, C., and T. Saevi (2009). 'An Event in Sound. Considerations on the Ethical-Aesthetic Traits of the Hermeneutic Phenomenological Text'. *Phenomenology & Practice*, 3 (1), 35–58.

Hogrebe, W. (2009). *Riskante Lebensnähe. Die szenische Existenz des Menschen.* Berlin: Akademie Verlag.

Honnef-Becker, I., and P. Kühn (2019). *Sprechen und Zuhören im Deutschunterricht. Bildungsstandards – Didaktik – Unterrichtsbeispiele.* Tübingen: Narr.

hooks, b. (1989). *Talking Back. Thinking Feminist. Thinking Black.* Boston: South End Press.

Hopkins, B. C. (2023). 'The Problem of the Unity of a Manifold in the Development of Husserl's Philosophy'. In J. Yoshimi, Ph. Walsh and P. Londen (eds), *Horizons of Phenomenology. Essays on the State of the Field and Its Applications.* Contributions to Phenomenology 122. Cham: Springer, 81–106. Available online: https://doi.org/10.1007/978-3-031-26074-2 (accessed 19 December 2023).

Husserl, E. (1939). 'Die Frage nach dem Ursprung der Geometrie als intentional-historisches Problem'. In E. Fink (ed.), *Revue internationale de Philosophie*, 1 (2), 203–25.

Husserl, E. ([1936] 1970). *The Crisis of European Sciences and Transcendental Phenomenology. An Introduction to Phenomenological Philosophy.* Translated by D. Carr. Evanston: Northwestern University Press.

Husserl, E. ([1931] 1982). *Cartesian Meditations. An Introduction to Phenomenology.* Translated by D. Cairns. Seventh impression. The Hague: Martinus Nijhoff.

Husserl, E. ([1859–1938] 1989). *Ideas Pertaining to a Pure Phenomenology and to a Phenomenlogical Philosophy. Second Book: Studies in the Phenomenology of Constitution.* Translated by R. Rojcewicz and A. Schuwer. Dordrecht: Kluwer Academic.

Husserl, E. ([1928] 1991). *On the Phenomenology of the Consciousness of Internal Time (1893–1917).* Translated by J. B. Brough. Dordrecht: Kluwer Academic.

Husserl, E. ([1900–1] 2001a). *Logical Investigations. Vol. 1.* Translated by J. N. Findlay from the Second German edition of Logische Untersuchungen, edited by D. Moran. London: Routledge.

Husserl, E. ([1900–1] 2001b). *Logical Investigations. Vol. 2.* Translated by J. N. Findlay from the Second German edition of Logische Untersuchungen, edited by D. Moran. London: Routledge.

Husserl, E. ([1913] 2014). *Ideas for a Pure Phenomenology and Phenomenological Philosophy. First Book: General Introduction to Pure Phenomenology.* Translated by D. O. Dahlstrom. Indianapolis: Hackett.

Hyle, A., M. Ewing, D. Montgomery and J. Kaufman (2008). *Dissecting the Mundane. International Perspectives on Memory-Work*. Lanham: University Press of America.
Krell, D. F. (1982). 'Phenomenology of Memory from Husserl to Merleau-Ponty'. *Philosophy and Phenomenological Research*, 42 (4), 492–505.
Jaeger, M., and K. Karlson (2018). *Cultural Capital and Educational Inequality: A Counterfactual Analysis*. Sociological Science, 5 (33), 775–95. Available online: https://doi.org/10.15195/v5.a33 (accessed 22 December 2023).
Klafki, W. (2007). *Neue Studien zur Bildungstheorie und Didaktik. Zeitgemäße Allgemeinbildung und kritisch-konstruktive Didaktik.* 6th edition. Weinheim: Beltz.
Kockelmans, J. J. (ed.) (1987). *Phenomenological Psychology: The Dutch School*. Dordrecht: Kluwer.
Krenn, S. (2017a). *Ergriffen sein im Lernprozess. Über die prägende Wirkung von Schule als Erfahrungsraum*. Bad Heilbrunn: Klinkhardt.
Krenn, S. (2017b). 'Das erfreuliche Ereignis – freundschaftliche Ergriffenheit'. In M. Ammann, T. Westfall-Greiter and M. Schratz (eds), *Erfahrungen deuten – Deutungen erfahren. Experiential Vignettes and Anecdotes as Research, Evaluation and Mentoring Tool*. Erfahrungsorientierte Bildungsforschung, vol. 3. Innsbruck: StudienVerlag, 179–82.
Krenn, S. (2020). 'Die Kunst des Anekdoten-Schreibens. Vom Gespräch zur Anekdote – Über das Verfassen von Anekdoten als Forschungsinstrument'. In H. K. Peterlini, I. Cennamo and J. Donlic (eds), *Wahrnehmung als pädagogische Übung. Theoretische und praxisorientierte Auslotungen einer phänomenologisch orientierten Bildungsforschung*. Erfahrungsorientierte Bildungsforschung, vol. 7. Innsbruck: StudienVerlag, 97–105.
Laing, R. D. (1967). *The Politics of Experience and the Bird of Paradise*. Westminster: Penguin Books.
Langdridge, D. (2008). 'Phenomenology and Critical Social Psychology: Directions and Debates in Theory and Research'. *Social and Personality Psychology Compass*, 2, 1126–42.
Langeveld, M. J. (1972). *Capita uit de algemene methodologie der opvoedingswetenschap*. Utrecht: Wolters-Noordhoff.
Lehner, D., and H. K. Peterlini (2020). 'Szenisches Mitfühlen als Sprache des Unterdrückten. Auslotung performativer Verstehensmöglichkeiten am Beispiel einer Vignette – ein Versuch'. In V. Symeonidis and J. F. Schwarz (eds), *Erfahrungen verstehen – (Nicht-)Verstehen erfahren. Potential und Grenzen der Vignetten- und Anekdotenforschung in der Annäherung an das Phänomen Verstehen*. Erfahrungsorientierte Bildungsforschung, vol. 8. Innsbruck: StudienVerlag, 91–101.

Leitner-Klaunzer, V. (2017). 'Mit der Natur befreundet'. In M. Ammann, T. Westfall-Greiter and M. Schratz (eds), *Erfahrungen deuten – Deutungen erfahren. Experiential Vignettes and Anecdotes as Research, Evaluation and Mentoring Tool*. Erfahrungsorientierte Bildungsforschung, vol. 3. Innsbruck: StudienVerlag, 177–8.

Lilienfeld, S. O., S. J. Lynn and J. M. Lohr (2014). *Science and Pseudoscience in Clinical Psychology. Initial Thoughts, Reflections, and Considerations*. 2nd edition. New York: Guilford.

Luccio, R. (1999). 'On Prägnanz'. In L. Albertazzi (ed.), *Shapes of Forms. From Gestalt Psychology and Phenomenology to Ontology and Mathematics*. Synthese Libraray 275. Dordrecht: Springer, 123–48.

Macnaughton, J. (1995). 'Anecdotes and Empiricism'. *British Journal of General Practice*, 45 (400), 571–2.

Merleau-Ponty, M. ([1964] 1968). *The Visible and the Invisible*. Edited by C. Lefort, translated by Alphonso Lingis. Evanston: Northwestern University Press.

Merleau-Ponty, M. (1970). *Themes from the Lectures at the Collège de France 1952–1960. Studies in Phenomenology & Existential Philosophy*. Translated by J. O'Neill. Evanston: Nortwestern University.

Merleau-Ponty, M. (1994). *Keime der Vernunft. Vorlesungen an der Sorbonne 1949–1952*. Edited by B. Waldenfels. München: Fink.

Merleau-Ponty, M. ([1945] 2005). *Phenomenology of Perception*. Translated by C. Smith. London: Routledge.

Meyer-Drawe, K. (1984). 'Grenzen pädagogischen Verstehens – Zur Unlösbarkeit des Theorie-Praxis-Problems in der Pädagogik'. Vierteljahresschrift für wissenschaftliche Pädagogik, 60 (3), 249–59.

Meyer-Drawe, K. (1996). 'Welt-Rätsel. Merleau-Pontys Kritik an Husserls Konzeption des Bewußtseins'. In *Phänomenologische Forschungen*, vol. 30, 194–221. Available online: https://www.jstor.org/stable/24360345 (accessed 2 January 2024).

Meyer-Drawe, K. (2008). *Diskurse des Lernens*. Munich: Fink.

Meyer-Drawe, K. (2012a). 'Vorwort'. In M. Schratz, J. F. Schwarz and T. Westfall-Greiter (eds), *Lernen als bildende Erfahrung. Vignetten in der Praxisforschung*. Innsbruck: StudienVerlag, 11–15.

Meyer-Drawe, K. (2012b). 'Gefangen in der Alltagswelt. Schattenseiten des selbstorganisierten Lernens'. In O. Dörner, B. Schäffer and M. Schemman (eds), *Erwachsenenbildung im Kontext. Theoretische Rahmungen, empirische Spielräume und praktische Regulative*. Vienna: Bertelsmann, 31–41.

Meyer-Drawe, K. (2020). 'Szenisches Verstehen'. In V. Symeonidis and J. F. Schwarz (eds), *Erfahrungen verstehen – (Nicht-)Verstehen erfahren*.

Potential und Grenzen der Vignetten- und Anekdotenforschung in der Annäherung an das Phänomen Verstehen. Erfahrungsorientierte Bildungsforschung, vol. 8. Innsbruck: StudienVerlag, 17–28.

Möltner, V. (2017). 'Freundschaft und Raum'. In M. Ammann, T. Westfall-Greiter and M. Schratz (eds), *Erfahrungen deuten – Deutungen erfahren. Experiential Vignettes and Anecdotes as Research, Evaluation and Mentoring Tool*. Erfahrungsorientierte Bildungsforschung, vol. 3. Innsbruck: StudienVerlag, 173–6.

Moran, D. (2000). *Introduction to Phenomenology*. London: Routledge.

Muchow, M. ([1935] 2012). *Der Lebensraum des Großstadtkindes. Mit Hans-Heinrich Muchow*. New edition by Imbke Behnken und Michael-Sebastian Honig. Weinheim: Juventa.

Nietzsche, F. ([1873] 1973). 'Die Philosophie im tragischen Zeitalter der Griechen'. In G. Colli and M. Montinari (eds), *F.N.: Werke. Nachgelassene Schriften 1870-1873*. Berlin: De Gruyter, 293–366.

Onions, C. T. (ed.) (1969). *The Oxford Dictionary of English Etymology*. Oxford: Clarendon.

Pessoa, F. (1989). *Alberto Caeiro – Dichtungen. Ricardo Reis – Oden*. Frankfurt/M.: Fischer.

Peterlini, H. K. (2016a). *Lernen und Macht. Prozesse der Bildung zwischen Autonomie und Abhängigkeit*. Erfahrungsorientierte Bildungsforschung, vol. 1. Innsbruck: StudienVerlag.

Peterlini, H. K. (2016b). 'Fenster zum Lernen. Forschungserfahrungen im Unterrichtsgeschehen – Einführung und Einblicke in die Suche nach einem neuen Verständnis von Lernen'. In S. Baur and H. K. Peterlini (eds), *An der Seite des Lernens*. Erfahrungsorientierte Bildungsforschung, vol. 2. Vienna: StudienVerlag, 21–9.

Peterlini, H. K. (2016c). '"So lange bis man's dann kann". Was Schülerinnen und Schüler von ihrem Lernen erzählen. Auszüge aus Interviews und Gruppengesprächen'. In S. Baur and H. K. Peterlini (eds), *An der Seite des Lernens*. Erfahrungsorientierte Bildungsforschung, vol. 2. Vienna: StudienVerlag, 169–200.

Peterlini, H. K. (2017). 'Die Geburt des Pathos. Performative Anstöße zu pädagogischen Verstehens- und Handlungsmöglichkeiten durch Vignetten, Zeichnungen und szenische Darbietung'. In M. Schratz, M. Ammann and T. Westfall-Greiter (eds), *Erfahrungen deuten – Deutungen erfahren. Experiental Vignettes and Anecdotes as Research, Evaluation and Mentoring Tool*. Erfahrungsorientierte Bildungsforschung, vol. 3. Innsbruck: StudienVerlag, 41–60.

Peterlini, H.K. (2019). 'Über den Abgrund der Dichotomie. Pädagogische Dilemmata und Perspektiven für einen neuen Umgang mit Natur und Erde'. In L. Dozza (ed.), *Io corpo – Io racconto – Io emozione*. Bergamo: Zeroseiup, 31–43.

Peterlini H. K (2020a). 'Phänomenologie als Forschungshaltung. Einführung in Theorie und Methodik für das Arbeiten mit Vignetten und Lektüren'. In J. Donlic and I. Straßer (eds), *Gegenstand und Methoden qualitativer Sozialforschung. Einblicke in die Forschungspraxis*. Opladen: Barbara Budrich, 121–38.

Peterlini, H. K. (2020b). 'Der zweifältige Körper. Die Leib-Körper-Differenz als diskriminierungskritische Perspektive. Vignettenforschung zu Rassismus, Sexismus und Behinderung'. In H. K. Peterlini, I. Cennamo and J. Donlic (eds), *Wahrnehmung als pädagogische Übung. Theoretische und praxisorientierte Auslotungen einer phänomenologisch orientierten Bildungsforschung*. Erfahrungsorientierte Bildungsforschung, vol. 7. Innsbruck: StudienVerlag, 25–45.

Peterlini, H. K. (2023). *Learning Diversity*. Wiesbaden: Springer.

Peterlini, H. K. (2024). 'Sozialität der Leiblichkeit. Phänomenologische Perspektiven auf Bildungsprozesse zwischen Subjekt und Welt'. In S. Blumenthal, A. Knecht, E. Kocnik, R. More and M. Sigot (eds), *Bildung: Sozial – informell – transformative. Festschrift für Stephan Sting*. Opladen: Barbara Budrich, 87–100.

Peterlini, H. K., E. Agostini, S. Krenn and G. Rathgeb (2021). '"Evidenzen" sichtbar machen: Messen und Bewerten als Dilemma eines komplexen Machtgeschehens'. In D. Kemethofer, J. Reitinger and K. Soukup-Altrichter (eds), *Vermessen? Zum Verhältnis von Bildungsforschung, Bildungspolitik und Bildungspraxis*. Beiträge zur Bildungsforschung, vol. 7. Münster: Waxmann, 110–26.

Peterlini, H. K., I. Cennamo and J. Donlic (eds) (2020). *Wahrnehmung als pädagogische Übung. Theoretische und praxisorientierte Auslotungen einer phänomenologisch orientierten Bildungsforschung*. Erfahrungsorientierte Bildungsforschung, vol. 7. Innsbruck: Studienverlag.

Peterlini H. K., J. Donlic, E. Imširović, I. Lippitz, V. Reumüller. P. Schlögl, J. Stopper and F. Waller (2023). *Perspektiven auf Beweggründe und Barrieren für oder gegen die Aufnahme eines Hochschulstudiums. Forschungsbericht*. Available online: https://doi.org/10.13140/RG.2.2.30682.72648 (accessed 22 December 2023).

Peterlini H. K., J. Donlic, J. Stopper, E. Imsirovic, I. Lippitz, V. Reumüller, S. Schönberg and I. Winter (2022). 'BildungsUtopien im Übergang? Mentoring als Ressource für einen chancengerechten Hochschulzugang von First Generation Students'. In M. Pissarek, M. Wieser, J. Koren, V. Kucher and V. Novak-Geiger (eds), *Projektbezogene Kooperation: von Schule und Universität. Synergien, Gelingensbedingungen, Evaluation*. Münster: Waxmann, 205–22.

Raab, J., M. Pfadenhauer, P. Stegmaier, J. Dreher and B. Schnettler (2008). 'Einleitung der Herausgeber. Phänomenologie und Soziologie. Grenzbestimmung eines Verhältnisses'. In J. Raab, M. Pfadenhauer, P. Stegmaier, J. Dreher and B. Schnettler (eds), *Phänomenologie und Soziologie. Theoretische Positionen, aktuelle Problemfelder und empirische Umsetzungen*. Wiesbaden: VS Verlag für Sozialwissenschaften, 11–32.

Rathgeb, G. (2017). 'Freundschaft als Kompetenz?'. In M. Ammann, T. Westfall-Greiter and M. Schratz (eds), *Erfahrungen deuten – Deutungen erfahren. Experiential Vignettes and Anecdotes as Research, Evaluation and Mentoring Tool*. Erfahrungsorientierte Bildungsforschung, vol. 3. Innsbruck: StudienVerlag, 167–8.

Rathgeb, G. (2023). 'Phänomenologische Pädagogik'. In M. Huber and M. Döll (ed.), *Bildungswissenschaft in Begriffen, Theorien und Diskursen*. Wiesbaden: Springer, 443–50.

Rathgeb, G., S. Krenn and M. Schratz (2017). 'Erfahrungen zum Ausdruck verhelfen'. In M. Ammann, T. Westfall-Greiter and M. Schratz (eds), *Erfahrungen deuten – Deutungen erfahren. Experiential Vignettes and Anecdotes as Research, Evaluation and Mentoring Tool*. Erfahrungsorientierte Bildungsforschung, vol. 3. Innsbruck: StudienVerlag, 125–51.

Revelant, A. (2023). *Macht und Hierarchie. Erfahrungen von Mitarbeiterinnen und Mitarbeitern aus sozialpädagogischen Einrichtungen mit stationärem Setting*. Klagenfurt-Celovec: Universität Klagenfurt.

Ricœur, P. (1985). *Time and Narrative*, vol. 3. Translated by Kathleen Blamey and David Pellauer. Chicago: University Chicago Press.

Roth, H. (1971). *Pädagogische Anthropologie. Entwicklung und Erziehung. Grundlagen einer Entwicklungspödagogik*. Stuttgart: Klett.

Rother, C. (2002). 'Die Unvollständigkeit der Reduktion. Metaphorik bei Husserl und bei Merleau-Ponty'. In M. Asiáin, H. Eckl and H. J. Pieper (eds), *Der Grund, die Not und die Freude des Bewußtseins. Beiträge zum Internationalen Symposion in Venedig zu Ehren von Wolfgang Marx*. Würzburg: Königshausen & Neumann, 75–87.

Savin-Baden, M., and K. Wimpenny (2014). *A Practical Guide to Arts-Related Research*. Wiesbaden: Springer.

Schapp, W. (2004). *In Geschichten verstrickt. Zum Sein von Mensch und Ding*. Frankfurt a. M.: Klostermann.

Schmitz, H. (1990). *Der unerschöpfliche Gegenstand. Grundzüge der Philosophie*. Bonn: Bouvier.

Schmitz, H. (2019). *New Phenomenology. A Brief Introduction*. With an introduction by Tonino Griffero. Translated by Rudolf Owen

Müllan with support from Martin Bastert. Milan-Udine: Mimesis International.

Schratz, M. (2015). '"Ein Eigenwilliges System ..." oder: SCHULe-MIT-WIRKUNG. Die Gesamtschule Barmen, Wuppertal'. In M. Schratz, H. A. Pant and B. Wischer (eds), *Was für Schulen! Unterrichtsqualität – Beispiele guter Praxis*. Seelze: Kallmeyer-Klett, 27–35.

Schratz, M. (2017). 'Schule ist mehr als die Summe des Unterrichts'. In M. Ammann, T. Westfall-Greiter and M. Schratz (eds), *Erfahrungen deuten – Deutungen erfahren. Experiential Vignettes and Anecdotes as Research, Evaluation and Mentoring Tool*. Erfahrungsorientierte Bildungsforschung, vol. 3. Innsbruck: StudienVerlag, 169–71.

Schratz, M., J. F. Schwarz and T. Westfall-Greiter (2012). *Lernen als bildende Erfahrung. Vignetten in der Praxisforschung. Mit einem Vorwort von Käte Meyer-Drawe und Beitragen von Carol Ann Tomlinson, Mike Rose und Horst Rumpf*. Innsbruck: StudienVerlag.

Schrittesser, I., and K. Witt-Löw (2022). *Schulgeschichten in der Lehrer:innenbildung. Über den Einsatz kollektiver Erinnerungsarbeit in der Lehrerinnen- und Lehrerbildung*. Bad Heilbrunn: Klinkhardt.

Slotnick, S. D. (2012). 'The Cognitive Neuroscience of Memory'. *Cognitive Neuroscience*, 3 (3–4), 139–41. Available online: https://doi.org/10.1080/17588928.2012.696536 (accessed 5 January 2024).

Smith, J. A. (2004). 'Reflecting on the Development of Interpretative Phenomenological Analysis and Its Contribution to Qualitative Research in Psychology'. *Qualitative Research in Psychology*, 1 (1), 39–54.

Sontag, S. (1966). *Against Interpretation*. New York: Farrar, Straus and Giroux.

Spradley, J. P. (1980). *Participant Observation*. Orlando: Harcourt College, 58–62.

Steinbock, A. J. (1997). 'Back to the Things Themselves', in *Human Studies*, 20 (2), 127–35.

Stevenson, A. (2010). *Oxford Dictionary of English*. 3rd edition. Oxford: Oxford University Press.

Tengelyi, L. (2007). *Erfahrung und Ausdruck. Phänomenologie im Umbruch bei Husserl und Seinen Nachfolgern*. Dordrecht: Springer.

Thompson. W. N. (1975). *Aristotle's Deduction and Induction*. Amsterdam: Rodopi.

Upton, T. V. (1981). 'A Note on Aristotelian epagōgē'. *Phronesis*, 26 (2), 172–6. Available online: http://www.jstor.org/stable/4182121 (accessed 5 December 2023).

Van Manen, M (1989). 'By the Light of Anecdote'. *Phenomenology + Practice*, 7, 232–53.

Van Manen, M. (1990). *Researching Lived Experience. Human Science for an Action Sensitive Pedagogy*. Albany: State University of New York Press.
Van Manen, M. (1997). *Researching Lived Experience*. Ontario: Althouse Press.
Van Manen, M. (2002). *Writing in the Dark. Phenomenological Studies in Interpretive Inquiry*. London: Althouse Press.
Van Manen, M. (2007). 'Phenomenology of Practice'. *Phenomenology & Practice*, 1 (1), 11–30.
Van Manen, M. (2016). *Phenomenology of Practice. Meaning-Giving Methods in Phenomenological Research and Writing*. Walnut Creek, CA: Left Coast Press.
Van Manen, M., and M. van Manen (2021a). 'Doing Phenomenological Research and Writing'. *Qualitative Health Research*, 31 (6), 1069–82. https://doi.org/10.1177/10497323211003058 (accessed 4 January 2024).
Van Manen, M., and M. van Manen (eds) (2021b). *Classic Writings for a Phenomenology of Practice*. New York: Routledge.
Waldenfels, B. (2000). *Das leibliche Selbst. Vorlesungen zur Phänomenologie des Leibes*. Frankfurt/M.: Suhrkamp.
Waldenfels, B. (2007a). *Antwortregister*. Frankfurt/M.: Suhrkamp.
Waldenfels, B. (2007b). *The Question of the Other*. Albany: SUNY Press.
Waldenfels, B. (2011). *Phenomenology of the Alien. Basic Concepts*. Translated by A. Kozin and T. Stähler. Evanston: Northwestern University Press.
Wertz, F. (2005). 'Phenomenological Research Methods for Counselling Psychology. *Journal of Counselling Psychology*, 52 (2), 167–77.
Yıldız, E. (2020). *Ideen zu einer transreligiösen Bildung. Kontrapunktische Betrachungen. In Interreligöse Bildung zwischen Kontigenzbewusstsein. und Wahrheitsansprüchen*. Edited by Zekirija Sejdini and Martina Kraml. Stuttgart: Kohlhammer, 15–26.
Zill, R. (2014). 'Minima Historia. Die Anekdote als Philosophische Form'. *Zeitschrift für Ideengeschichte*, 8 (3), 33–46.

INDEX

Note: Endnotes are indicated by the page number followed by "n" and the endnote number e.g., 20 n.1 refers to endnote 1 on page 20.

Adams, Henry F. 6
Agostini, Evi 5, 10, 20, 24, 26, 86, 87, 97, 104, 114
Albertazzi, Liliana 38
Alexander the Great 9
Alvesson, Mats 94
ambiguity 12, 20, 44, 92, 93, 104, 105
Ammann, Markus 13, 43, 76, 81, 86, 88, 108, 120, 122
analysis
   conversation 14
   deconstruction 14
   discourse 14
   in-depth hermeneutic 14
   linguistic 14
   narrative 14
   narrative hermeneutic 14
   qualitative content 14
Ancient Greek 6, 32
anecdotes as a scientific tool 67
anonymity 101, 136, 139
apprenticeship 24, 122
Arbeitsgruppe Bielefelder Soziologen 13, 59
Arendt, Hannah 50, 89, 90
Aristotle 8–9, 19
Arrighetti, Graziano 8, 19, 28
Assmann, Aleida 42

Assmann, Jan 42
association 90
audio recordings 18, 29, 56, 59, 68, 82
Austrian Science Fund (FWF) 23, 30 n.2, 116 n.3
Austro-Hungarian Empire 130

Bachelard, Gaston 112
banality of evil 89, 90
Barthes, Roland 81
Beekmann, Ton 47
Bell, Beverley 7
Bengtsson, Jan 34
Bielefelder Soziologen 13, 59
biography 119, 131–3, 140
Blumenberg, Hans 28
Boal, Augusto 104
bodily expressions 25, 26, 48, 49, 68, 86, 97, 104, 107, 128
bodily interactivity 19, 73
bodily resonance 107
bodily speech 10, 138
body 5, 16, 17, 33, 36, 45–52, 59, 76, 82, 95, 106, 121, 139
   importance of 64–67
Bourdieu, Pierre 123, 124, 127
Bozzi, Paolo 41
bricolage 14

Brinkmann, Malte 14, 17, 55, 57, 58
Brinkmann, Svend 14, 17, 55, 57, 58
Brothers Grimm 6

Calvino, Italo 87, 90, 91
Carinthia 131, 133
case history 114
casuistry 26
Cennamo, Irene 10, 13, 18, 20, 60, 63
children 17, 40, 47, 49, 59, 105, 109, 110, 129, 130, 133, 137, 138
co-experience 18, 20, 21 n.2, 23, 26, 27, 56, 89, 98
 conversational turns from 75–9
 in the perspective of body and responsivity 45–52
co-experienced experience 47–8
cognition 8, 10, 33, 34, 36
collective memory work 28–9
compost narratives 29–30
comprehension 41
concentration camp 13, 88–90
confrontational approach 101
constructivism 14
conversations 1, 2, 5, 11, 12, 14, 25–7, 29, 31, 34–7, 45, 48–52, 73, 85, 92, 94, 97–100, 105, 114, 126–30, 136, 139, 140
 anecdote 67–72
 body and response 64–7
 from co-experience 75–9
 experience-orientated research 20
 impromptu 58–64
 and interview 55–8
 one experience, one theme and one focus 79–80
 phenomenologically orientated research 16–18

corporeality 36, 50, 51, 107
Costello, Peter R. 50
creativity 93
cultural heritage 131
cultural studies 14, 15

Dahlstrom, Michael F. 7, 8
Danner, Helmut 63
De Boer, Theo 8, 9
Denzin, Norman K. 7
dialect 68, 129
dialogical reading (partner reading) 101
Dickens, Charles 41
Diogenes 9
disadvantage 123–8
discrimination 60, 61, 130, 133, 136
documentary methods 14
Doing Interviews (Brinkmann and Kvale) 55
Donlic, Jasmin 10, 13, 18, 20, 60, 63, 131–3

earth stories 29
education 2, 24, 25, 37, 46, 109–13, 119, 121, 123–8, 133
Eichmann, Adolf 89
eidetic reduction 32, 34, 91
Eloff, Irma 5, 10, 24, 26
empathizing 90, 106, 107
epagogy 8
epistemology 34, 36, 46, 87
epoché 32, 34, 57
ethnographic methods 25
etymology 6
event of sound 73, 74
exclusion 127
exemplary discussion 101

facial expressions 16, 17, 50, 68, 76, 82, 83, 121, 128
Faulstich, Peter 59

Faulstich-Wieland, Hannelore 59
Finlay, Linda 92, 93
Flores D'Arcais, Paolo 10
focus groups 14, 43, 58, 59, 76, 77, 79, 122
Freud, Sigmund 41, 42, 45
friendship 84, 108–11, 113–15
Friesen, Norm 116 n.4
Fuchs, Thorsten 29

Gadamer, Hans 87, 93, 94, 97
Gehring, Petra 46
generalities 19
Gestalt psychology 38, 40
gestures 16, 41, 59, 63, 68, 104–7, 125
Giddens, Anthony 111
Giorgi, Amedeo 92, 93
Goethe, Johann Wolfgang von 91, 116 n.1
Gossman, Lionel 7
grounded theory 14
Gutzen, Dieter 6

habitus 127
Halbwachs, Maurice 41, 42
Hall, Stuart 133
Hamm, Robert 29
haptic aspect 121
Haraway, Donna 29–30
Haug, Frigga 28–29
Heidegger, Martin 74, 93
Hennigfeld, Iris 116 n.1
Henriksson, Carina 19, 26, 73–5, 81
hermeneutic learning 114
hermeneutics 14, 34, 63, 75, 87, 114
heterogenous groups 23
higher education 123, 127
history 2, 8, 13, 23, 25, 29, 30, 37, 88, 92, 114, 141
Hogrebe, Wolfram 12

Holocaust 88–90
Honnef-Becker, Irmgard 15
hooks, bell 133
Hopkins, Burt C. 11, 41, 44
hospital 59, 134, 138
humanities 119, 128–31
Humboldt University Berlin 104
Husserl, Edmund 7–12, 31, 32, 34–8, 44, 51, 52, 57, 75, 86, 87, 94
Hyle, Adrienne E. 29

identity building 131–3
intercorporeality 50, 51, 107
interexperience, concept of 48
International Symposium on Phenomenological Educational Science 104
inter-religiosity 132
interviews 1, 2, 5, 11, 12, 14, 16–18, 20, 23, 24, 26, 60, 67, 68, 76, 82, 103, 128, 132, 133, 136, 140
  conversation and 55–8
Italy 129–31

Jaeger, Mads Meier 123

Kant, Immanuel 34, 44, 94
Karlson, Kristian 123
Keller, Mitra 76, 78
Klafki, Wolfgang 109
Kockelmans, Joseph J. 74
Köhler, Wolfgang 40
Krell, David Farell 37, 44, 48
Krenn, Silvia 12, 16, 17, 19, 24, 69, 72, 108, 114, 115
Kühn, Peter 15
Kvale, Steinar 14, 17, 55, 58

Laing, Ronald D. 47, 48
Langdridge, Darren 93
Latin 32

Lehner, Daniela 105, 106, 116 n.2
Leitner-Klaunzer, Verena 108
lifeworlds 1, 14, 25, 75, 112, 128, 140
Lilienfeld, Scott O. 7
literary studies 6, 91
lived experience 10, 11, 18, 19, 25, 26, 31, 35, 36, 38, 41, 65–7, 72–5, 92, 101
Locke, John 37
Lohr, Jeffrey 7
Lynn, Steven J. 7

Macnaughton, Jane 7, 134
Mauthausen 13, 88–90, 106
memory
  collective 28–9, 41, 42
  communicative 42
  cultural 42
  culture 131
  individual 41, 42
  mimetic 42
  social 41
Merleau-Ponty, Maurice 1, 32, 33, 36, 42, 43, 45, 46, 48, 49, 51
methodological approach 14, 68, 114
Meyer-Drawe, Käte 19, 20, 26, 36, 37, 39, 106, 107, 110, 111, 116 n.4
migration 114, 115, 130, 131
mimicry 41
Möltner, Veronika 108
Moran, Dermot 92
Muchow, Hans-Heinrich 59
Muchow, Martha 59
Muslims 131, 133

narrative style 15, 80
new secondary school (NMS – Neue Mittelschule) 23, 24, 30 n.1, 72, 109, 111, 113
Nietzsche, Friedrich 8, 28

non-academic families 123
nonconceptuality, theory of 28
nous 8

Oellers, Norbert 6
oikos 113
Onions, Charles Talbut 6
Oxford English Dictionary 6

Palomar, Mr 87, 90
participant experience 47
Passeron, Jean Claude 123
pathic 1, 20, 26
pedagogy 63, 119, 137
personal learning 23
Pessoa, Fernando 92
Peterlini, Hans Karl 5, 10, 13, 18, 20, 35, 46–8, 59, 60, 63, 86, 97, 103–6, 116 n.2, 123, 127, 128, 130, 138
Petersen, Jürgen H. 6
phenomenological lifeworld analysis 14
phenomenological surplus 69, 94, 97, 113, 140
phenomenology 1, 2, 8, 9, 11, 28, 31–4, 36–8, 44, 46, 48, 75, 87, 92, 93, 141
phenomenon 32, 35, 41, 57, 58, 66, 69, 75, 93, 94, 104, 115
  of alienness 51
  of angels 33
philosophical system 9, 28
PhotoVoice Method 132
plurilogical reading (group reading) 98, 100–3
'pointing out' 91–7
'pointing to' 91–7
Polytechnic School 138 n.1
posture 16, 17, 49, 50, 68, 82, 83, 104–6
power relations 42, 63, 135
prejudice 40, 41, 127

INDEX

prior knowledge 18, 20, 89, 94, 95, 114, 115
privilege 37, 123–8
professional development 7, 25, 100, 119, 137–8
professional settings 137
Proust, Marcel 49
psychoanalysis 41, 42
psychotherapy 15
punchline 12, 19, 24, 73, 79, 82, 83, 98
punctum 20, 80, 81

question guide 56, 58, 65

Raab, Jürgen 91
Rathgeb, Gabriele 2, 12, 16, 17, 19, 24, 108, 113, 114
raw anecdote 73, 82–4
recording 12, 17, 18, 29, 56, 59, 65, 67, 68, 107
reflection 5, 7, 10, 11, 14, 24, 25, 33, 38, 45, 51, 57, 63, 85, 86, 90, 91, 97, 103, 106, 108, 113, 115, 119, 121, 131, 134–8
relationships 16–18, 23, 24, 41, 45, 64, 66, 75, 78, 92, 110–15, 125, 139
religion 15, 33, 131–3
remembered experiences 16, 18–20, 25, 26, 29, 34, 35, 44, 49, 65, 76, 79, 80, 83, 89, 94, 114, 115, 141
research
 anecdote 1, 2, 5, 6, 8, 9, 11, 12, 14, 17, 18, 20, 23, 26, 29–31, 37, 43, 45, 47–9, 51, 55–8, 64, 65, 75, 86, 92, 94, 100, 102, 104, 105, 119, 121, 123, 128, 131, 132, 135, 139–41
 biographical 29, 63
 educational 11, 37
 ethnographic 119, 128–31

generational 37
groups 24, 56, 73, 82–4, 98, 107, 108, 113, 120
myth 37
phenomenological 5, 10, 31–3, 37, 40, 57, 59, 75, 85, 92–4, 101, 106, 141
social 37, 91
socio-spatially orientated 131
vignette 5, 10, 25–7, 58, 59, 85, 119
resonance readings 14, 20, 85, 88, 89, 93, 103, 138
 as academic text 107–13
Revelant, Alina 50, 135
Ricœur, Paul 86, 87
river of experience 16
Roth, Heinrich 109
Rother, Carsten 32

Saevi, Tone 19, 26, 73–5, 81
Sandberg, Jörgen 94
Savin-Baden, Maggi S. 7
scenic reading 103–7, 116 n.2
Schapp, Wilhelm 15
Schmitz, Hermann 33–4
school 1, 13, 23, 25, 32, 35, 43, 57, 81–3, 101, 103, 108–10, 112, 114, 119, 125, 127
 as an institution 122
 experiences and educational biographies 99
 learning 69, 121
 learning and teaching in 120–3
 learning experiences 69
 phenomenological research practice 93
Schratz, Michael 5, 10, 12, 16, 17, 19, 24, 26, 86, 97, 108, 110–14, 116 n.3
Schwarz, Johanna F. 26, 86
sedimentation 11, 44, 45
self-image 84

sensory perception 7, 46, 91
shapes 39
Slotnick, Scott D. 37
Smith, Jonathan A. 93
social conditions 29, 123, 127
social sciences 28, 119, 128–31
Sontag, Susan 91
South Tyrol 129, 130
Spradley, James P. 47
Steinbock, Anthony J. 31, 33
stereotypes 106, 130, 133
Stevenson, Angus 32
Stoa 32
storytelling 14–16, 26, 77, 128, 140
Swann's Way (Proust) 49
symbolic interactionism 14

teacher education 99
teaching in schools 120–3
Tengelyi, László 12, 16
theory of memory 41, 44
Thompson, Wayne 8
tone of voice 41, 50, 67, 76, 82, 83, 126
transcription 17, 56, 59, 67–72, 79
transcripts 12, 18, 24, 25, 29, 56, 68, 82

unconscious 45, 46, 97, 99

University of Innsbruck 5, 23, 58
University of Klagenfurt 123, 129, 131, 138 n.2
University of Vienna 125
Upton, Thomas V. 8

validation 36, 73, 82–4, 98, 107, 136
van Manen, Max 8–11, 17, 18, 24, 27–8, 31, 32, 36, 57, 66, 67, 74–6, 80, 81
van Manen, Michael 36
The Visible and the Invisible (Merleau-Ponty) 33
visualization 45, 71

Waldenfels, Bernhard 17, 51, 52, 64, 65, 116 n.4
Wallace, Rachel x
Wertz, Frederick J. 92
Westfall-Greiter, Tanja 26, 86, 108
Wimpenny, Katherine 7
workshops 100, 101, 136
World War II 130
Writing in the Dark (Van Manen) 19, 74

Yildiz, Erol 131, 133

Zill, Rüdiger 28